Harry Lyman Koopman

Orestes

A Dramatic Sketch And Other Poems

Harry Lyman Koopman

Orestes
A Dramatic Sketch And Other Poems

ISBN/EAN: 9783744704809

Printed in Europe, USA, Canada, Australia, Japan

Cover: Foto ©Thomas Meinert / pixelio.de

More available books at **www.hansebooks.com**

ORESTES
A DRAMATIC SKETCH AND OTHER POEMS
BY HARRY LYMAN KOOPMAN

BUFFALO, N. Y.
MOULTON, WENBORNE & CO.
1888.

TO MY KINSMAN AND FRIEND,
REUBEN HARVEY MITCHELL
OF FREEPORT, MAINE.

ERRATA.

Page 56, line 9, "Again *not* "Again"
" 58, " 19, half *not* so
" 66, " 31, Getting *not* g
" 74, " 26, ruth *not* truth
" 88, " 23, the *not* tfle
" 99, " 12, shop *not* shops
" 110, " 10, wonderland *not* wouderful
" 111, " 14, watchman *not* watching
" 118, " 22, laggards *not* laggard's
" 128, " 16, your *not* you
" 143, " 3, war, *not* war.
" 144, " 16, brought. *not* brought,
" 152, " 12, breath! *not* breath
" 153, " 20, light, *not* light.
" 155, " 24, to-day thou *not* thou
" 185, " 30, rétroussés. *not* retrousses.

Cousin Nell,
Criticism,
Crows, The, . . .
David's Lament over Saul and Jonathan,
Day Red, . . .
Dayspring, .
Death of Guinevere, The,

Page.
191
39
189
93
120
89
129
53
35
62
42
131
43
56
59
81
150
44
151
60
100
80
41
179
51
107
97
92
154
46
58
90
135
50
153
28

CONTENTS.

———o———

	Page.
Ad Socium,	191
Afterglow,	39
Angels' Visits,	189
Anniversary Hymn,	93
Antecedents,	120
Arrow Shot, An,	89
At My Northern Window,	129
Autumn,	53
Balder,	35
Barker, David,	62
Barred Out,	42
Beowulf, Foresong to,	131
Blindness,	43
Blush, A,	56
Boot and Saddle,	59
Booth, Edwin,	81
Brown, John,	150
Burden, The,	44
By the Sea,	151
Ça Ira,	60
Calm,	100
Camden Hills,	80
Champlain Glimpses,	41
Chestnut Bell, The,	179
Child of the Northern Star,	51
Children,	107
Christopher,	97
Coburn, Charles Miller,	92
Constitution, The,	154
Cousin Nell,	46
Criticism,	58
Crows, The,	90
David's Lament over Saul and Jonathan,	135
Day Red,	50
Dayspring,	153
Death of Guinevere, The,	28

Devil, The,	192
Difference, The,	62
Dudeling's Fate, The,	184
Earth School, The,	61
Ebeeme,	82
Ebeeme Boating Song,	85
Eldorado,	109
Emerson,	94
Epigæa Repens Coronata,	107
Estranged,	47
Evening,	101
Fallen,	100
Fated,	47
Fisherman, The,	188
Flowerless,	106
Frolic of the Leaves, The,	113
Frozen Waterfall, The,	81
Garfield,	99
Gauntlet, The,	143
German Love Song of the 12th Century,	141
Grant,	60
Great Admiral, The,	31
Hadrian, Dying, to His Soul,	136
Her Mind,	191
Heredity,	80
Hesper,	146
Homer, Translations from,	137
Humorous Poems,	171
Icarus,	42
Idun; or, The Meeting Ways,	157
Ilioneus,	145
In Boston Common,	89
In the Kingdom of the Blind,	40
In Tau Kappa Phi,	121
Isle au Haut,	49
Jonah,	191
King Death,	183
Landlady's Daughter, The,	141
Land-longing,	88
Lapland Driving Song,	78
Left Behind,	63
Life,	192
Lion of Lucerne, The,	143
Longfellow,	94
Loreley, The,	134
Lost,	96
Love,	102
Love in the Northland,	108
Love-Pains,	190

Love's Arrow,	128
Love's Faltering,	54
Lover's Oath, The,	190
Materialism,	63
May,	105
Miller's Songs of the Sierras,	144
Milton,	148
Morn,	101
Morning,	101
My Child Love,	57
My Galahad,	149
My Worship,	147
Norns, The,	70
Not the Same,	52
O Heart, and Must I Sing to Thee,	155
Old Mathematician, The,	104
Orestes; or, The Avenger,	7
Out of the Depths,	66
Out West,	189
Outshone,	154
Over Birth,	116
Pancakes,	178
Path to Songland, The,	116
Persistence,	142
Phosphor,	145
Pirate Horse-Car, The,	173
Poet, The,	119, 191
Poet and the Birds, The,	55
Poets,	41
Poet's Treasure, The,	86
Potencies,	154
Priceless,	146
Prince Henry to Elsie,	84
Princess Eyebright,	58
Purity,	99
Question, The,	43
Recompense,	119
Reform,	95
Rest,	50
Rhymes,	190
Rus Ivit,	152
Saint Elizabeth,	44
Sea and Shore,	34
Seasons, The,	48
Self-Deception,	62
Shepherdess Moon, The,	136
Sin,	102
Singer, The,	113
Small to the Great, The,	79

Song-Birth,	147
Soul and Body,	65
Springy,	190
Storm,	104
Success,	118
Summer Night in Winter, A,	69
Summer's Day, A,	150
Sunlight,	120
Swedenborg,	133
Temples,	123
Three Letters,	124
Three Stages, The,	19
To Princess Eyebright in the Catskills,	156
To the Firefly,	111
To the May-Flower,	87
Town Clock, The,	149
Truth,	102
Twelve Undertakers of Burlington, The,	180
Twofold Teaching, A,	103
Una Sanctarum,	152
Unconscious Beauty,	148
Unhidden,	53
Unthrift,	86
Vergil, Translations from,	140
Wanhope,	119
Wedlock,	39
Work and Wages,	187
World-Voice, The,	118

ORESTES

—OR—

THE ❖ AVENGER.

A DRAMATIC SKETCH.

Characters in the Play.

Agamemnon, king of Argos.

Ægisthus, his supplanter.

Orestes, son of Agamemnon.

Clytæmnestra, wife of Agamemnon, and afterwards of Ægisthus.

Electra, daughter of Agamemnon.

Pylades, son of Strophius, king of Phocis, and friend of Orestes.

Guards.

Scene—Before the royal palace at Mycenæ.

ACT I.

Agamemnon comes in.

AGAMEMNON.

Hail, halls of Atreus, which in happy hour
Once more mine eyes behold! Ancestral courts,
Which echoed to my infant shouts, where sported
Brothers with foster-brother, hail! Thou shining sky,
Gladly I greet thy soaring arch of blue.
Not such at Ilium bentest thou above,
With frost that froze men's hearts and rains that
 drowned ;
Nor such, ye winds that play among the flowers,
As when ye snatched the leaguer's tents away,
And tore the long ships from their anchors' arms.
" Farewell loved scenes, for Troy we bend the oar."
Such was our parting ten long years agone.
Ah me! how few of all that crossed the foam,
In those my hundred ships, were left to watch
The Argive hills prick through the weltering blue,
And, risen, lift the curving shore to sight,
Then sink beyond their pines! But, come though late,
Though few we come, yet on our prows we bring
Bright Victory perched, and, in our hollow ships,
For you, O shield-hung halls, we lead a train
Of Trojan captives meet to serve our state.

But why in welcome swing not the wide doors?
Why comes with shouts and greetings and strown
    flowers,
No faithful band? Flashed not my beacon fires
The news of my return? Hath some mishap
Withheld the steps of my swift messenger
I sent but now before me from the ships?
Why stirs no life within? But let me turn,
You, ye fair fields to view.   The same, the same!

    *Ægisthus and Clytæmnestra come out of the palace.
    They embrace; then come forward, Clytæmnestra on the
    right, Ægisthus on the left.*

Already swings the laborer's arm in tilth,
Already glows the sward.   No fields like those
About the home; for here dwell peace and love.
My royal wife!

            CLYTÆMNESTRA.

         Late comes my lord, but yet,
The gods be thanked, he has not come too late:
Nor do the Phrygian plains infold his form.
But why thus unattended comes my lord,
No herald sent before, no beacon fire
To bid make ready royal welcome for him?
Comes he alone of all?

      Ægisthus stabs Agamemnon in the back.
            AGAMEMNON.

      Oh! I am slain.
False foster-brother! False wife! Now I see.
Oh! why in fondness did I leave my guards,
To rush but on my doom?

CLYTÆMNESTRA.

Remember her
Thou slewest in Aulis.

AGAMEMNON.

Nay, think not to cloak
Thy crime with her sweet name. Thou wanton beast,
Small joy thou'lt win of thine adulterous bed;
For vengeance, vengeance, though it sleep, shall come.
My sword shall wreak it,—oh! I die. I die.
The world grows dark. Orestes, mine Orestes,
Forget not those that slew thy sire. Revenge!

Dies. His guards come in and catch sight of the dead body.

GUARDS.

Whose deed is this?

ÆGISTHUS.

Stand off! What, guardsmen, ho!

The body-guard of ÆGISTHUS comes in and the soldiers of AGAMEMNON fall back.

He lies here justly, bathed in his own blood,
The bloody-handed, most unnatural father,
False leader, faithless husband, treacherous friend.
It was not meet his breath again should taint
This Argive air. But, now the soul has fled,
I spare his wretched corse, and, where he fell,
I will erect a tomb in honor not
Of him, but of the throne that he dishonored.
Now to your posts.

ELECTRA comes in, leading ORESTES, and sees the body of her father.

Electra.

My father, O my father,
What hath befallen? O father, speak to me!

She flings herself upon the body.

His cheeks are white and cold.   He does not breathe.
There's blood upon the ground.   Speak, mother, tell
    me,
How comes he so?

She sees the blood upon Ægisthus's sword.

Is this thy work, O villain,
Thou traitor, coward, murderer of thy host?
How darest thou stand beside my mother there?
O mother, dearest mother, leave his side.
Nay, give me back my father; spare thy words.

Ægisthus.

It wants but little I should slay you both,
And end this cursed breed; but, for her sake
That bore you, I refrain.   Henceforth, however,
On peril of thy life let me not hear
That ready tongue of thine.   His life and thine
Depend upon thy silence.

Ægisthus and Clytæmnestra go into the palace.

Electra.

Kneel Orestes,
And, with thy hand upon thy father's brow,
Swear by his throne, his glory and his murder,
By the bright sun, the earth and the round sea,
Thy love of good men's praise, thy hope to thrive,
By thine own honor, and by all the gods,

If ever thou to manhood shalt attain,
To wreak revenge upon the guilty wretch
That slew thy sire, the King of Men.

ORESTES.

I swear.

ACT II.

Eight years later. The tomb of AGAMEMNON *appears before the palace.* ELECTRA *stands beside it.*

ELECTRA.

Two lives we lead, of waking and of sleep.
The sun goes down, the heaven's myriad eyes
Look out upon the closing eyes of men.
The spear of dawn dashes upon the crests
Of the cold hills, and shivers into light;
Then birds and beasts and men awake and rise.
But which is true life, what the bright sun gilds,
Or what the stars bedew with influences?
Say rather both are true, and are but each
Opposing sides of one reality;
And life moves on unchanged through glow or gloom,
As the boat dashes onward, now in sun,
And now in shadow of the sail, but still
Unchecked, unaltered, to its haven speeds.
My father! oh, how many a night and oft
Beside my couch thy shadow hath appeared,

When I with all the house in slumber lay!
But not as yesternight; always before
Thou camest cold and pale, with stony eyes,
And spakest with hollow voice, and criedst,
    "Revenge!"
While thy wounds bled afresh, until my heart,
Beating, awoke me with upstarting hair.
But this morn, oh! I woke with tears of joy.
The sun shone on my bed, and in his light,
I deemed I saw thee still, no longer gray,
And battle-worn, and cold and faint with wounds;
But, glowing in the ruddy flush of youth,
With springing step, and eyes that darted hope,
Thou badest rejoice, for all my ills are o'er.
I scarce since then have ceased to weep for joy:
And yet no joy I find, but only grief;
For daily grow the sorrows of our house.
The servants that my father chose are bowed
With heavier burdens—those the grave hath spared:
And daily swells his insolence that struts
Where strode in majesty the King of Men.
Orestes, brother, wilt thou never come?
Boy that these hands led forth and stole from death,
Sending by secret ways to Phocis far;
And there, intrusting to good Strophius,
Left thee to grow into thy father's self,
Till manhood and the consciousness of strength
Should drive thee back to rid earth of a wretch.
But still thou comest not, though surely now,
Long since, thy voice hath caught a deeper tone,
Thy head a prouder poise, unless, ah me!
Some ill hath happed,—a fever caught thee hence,

Or wild boar, hunted, turned and rent thy flesh,
Or swift steed thrown thee, or the chariot wheels,
Confounded, crushed thy form; or, no, not so!
Like Iliona's traitorous spouse, thy host
Hath broken faith, and slain both thee and me.
But if thou livest, and thine arm fails not,
Why yet delayest thou? Is life so sweet
Thou canst not risk it in so dear a cause?
Hast thou forgot thy vow? Hast thou forgot
Thy father's murdered form, the tyrant's boast
And fraud against thy life? Wrought I in vain?
Are all my tears to thee as if unwept,
My toils unborne, revilings unendured?
It cannot be! Thou art thy father's son.
And, if thou livest, even now art sped
To swoop in vengeance on that guilty head.

ACT III.

Ægisthus and Clytemnestra come out of the palace.

Ægisthus.

Something too long have I endured her spite.
I dread e'en for thy life; lest in her madness,
Still brooding over how her father fell,
As if he had not merited his death
And tenfold worse; and in her melancholy
At seeing not her brother,—prudent lad!
He knows where he is safe,—dreaming I know not

What wild hope that the race of Pleisthenes
Should mount my throne again,—I fear lest she,
In mad revenge, should seek thy life and mine.
By sleight or craft. I fear not for myself,
But deep I should regret if she achieved
So much as an attempt upon thy health.
I do not fear her, though I know her plots
To tamper with my guards, and though I know,
In lacking power to harm, she lacks not will.

CLYTÆMNESTRA.

I should be loath to part e'en from a child
Lost to all claim on love. Yet, though I share not
Thine over anxious fears for me, I deem
Foresight the truest wisdom in a king;
For in himself he bears about the life
Not only of himself but of his subjects:
And even trivial dangers are not slight
Endangering all at once. So, not in fear,
But in a wise precaution, it were well,
For us and for Electra, to bestow
Her hand in marriage on some far-come suitor.
Not few such have appeared.

ÆGISTHUS.

Talk not of that,
Of seeking out new hate, and, for one foe,
Winning a second, and therewith an army.
What profits me my throne, if still *he* lives
I slew to win it? Lives and is at hand
To claim it hourly; for while they live,
His children, Agamemnon walks the earth.

CLYTÆMNESTRA.

What meanest thou?

ÆGISTHUS.

I would with this same steel
Make good my kingship that I won it with.

CLYTÆMNESTRA.

Thou wouldst not slay her!

ÆGISTHUS.

Even with this sword,
Beside her father's grave; so that, at last,
(For, of her brother, if indeed he live,
I take no thought), my throne might be secure,
Thy life be freed from risk, and, from the land
The memory of Atreus' line be razed.
A huntsman slew a tiger by its lair,
And found its cub within, and pitied it,
And brought it home. It played about the house,
Like any kitten, till its claws were grown,
Then, one fine morning, being fain of flesh,
It sprang upon its master, and devoured
The hand that nursed it. I would 'scape such fate.

CLYTÆMNESTRA.

So be it as thou wilt. Both daughters gone!
Ah me, how one deed draws another on!

ACT IV.

Guards before the palace.

1st Guard.

The king's at meat, and we before his doors
Must hold our watch.   At feasting, feasting still!
And up the chimney flies the savory smell
Of roast and sodden beast and bird and fish,
By many a starving hunter's peril caught;
But of it all the poor man wins no more
Than yon same chimney-bounty flung to air.
Ah! many a long year have the poor forgotten
The pathway to these doors; preferring ills
Of hunger, nakedness, cold and weariness,
Under the open sky, to blows and curses
At palace gates.

2d Guard.

   It was not always so.
There was a time when lameness leaped with joy
At sight of these same smokes; and nakedness
Was clad and sheltered in expectancy
Before it reached these halls; nor only so,
But found its hope of bounty realized,
Even upon the threshold.

Pylades enters.

   Who comes here?

Pylades.

Is this the palace of great Agamemnon?

3D GUARD.

It was; but now Ægisthus reigns instead.

PYLADES.

Ægisthus? I had thought the line of Atreus
Still held dominion o'er the Argive land.

3D GUARD.

Thou must have come from far not to have known
The ills—the changes—that have happened here.

PYLADES.

The ills?

3D GUARD.

I said not so. The word slipped out.
I meant no slander 'gainst my lord, the king.

PYLADES.

It matters not; but are the times so changed
From what they were when great Atreides lived?
Ruled the great king as one that loved his land?

GUARDS.

Ay! so he ruled.

PYLADES.

But did he leave no son
To follow in his steps and to receive
The scepter from his hand?

1ST GUARD.

A son he left,
But if he live we know not. Long ago,
He to the Phocian land far off was borne.

PYLADES.

The Phocian land! The prince's name?

1ST GUARD.

Orestes.

PYLADES.

Ah, hapless youth! Long since the tale was told
Of his young death. But, how he died I know not,
Whether by hostile steel, or fang of boar,
Turned in the breathless hunt, or in the crush
Of chariot-wheels confused with trampling hoofs,
Or in the treacherous wave: but this I know:
The Phocian air no more shall fan his cheek.

2D GUARD.

Woe, woe, and woe on woe! Unhappy Atreus,
Thy race is at an end. No more thy sons
With firm but gentle rule shall sway the land.
The blow that slew Atreides slew thy line.

PYLADES.

Yet were it that Orestes had not died,
Would there now be in Argos loyal hearts
To welcome him, and win his throne for him?

GUARDS.

Ay! Ay!

PYLADES.

Oh, that the grave might yield its prey,
Restore thee to the light, ill-starred Orestes!

ORESTES *enters and advances to his father's tomb. The guards start back.*

GUARDS.

A miracle! The gods have given back
Not young Orestes, but the King of Men.

> ORESTES, *without heeding them, cuts off a lock of his hair, and lays it upon his father's tomb.*

ORESTES.

Thou god that rulest the gloomy underworld,
Grant that my father's murder be avenged
By me, this day. Ye gods that sit above,
And mete out bliss and woe to mortal kind,
Give me to-day to gain my father's throne.
So will I rule, as he ruled, in the fear
Of all the gods, and in goodwill to men.

> *To the guards.*

Behold your king! Alas, that I so speak,
Not he that lies beneath! The gods rule all.
Will ye here serve me as ye served my sire
At Ilium, when the Trojan shafts fell thick,
And the ground shook with shock of trampling steeds,
And gods, contending, clouded all the air?

GUARDS.

Ay, king! Our hearts, our arms are thine. Lead on!

ORESTES.

Not yet. I'd slay the villain where he slew
My father, by this grave. Withdraw, but stand
To come at call. If he should call you, come;
He doubtless will find need, if not its help.

> *They go out.*

ACT V.

ELECTRA, *coming out of the palace, sings.*

ELECTRA.

Smile out, thou sun, in splendor,
   And gild the violet's bloom.
Till all its blossoms render
   Their homage of perfume :

But be thy beams withholden
   From eyes that weep like mine,
For suns that shone of olden,
   And nevermore shall shine.

Come rather thou, uncheery,
   Dark winter of my choice,
With freezing winds a-weary,
   That lend the midnight voice :

And, while thy snows drift over
   The forest's fallen pride,
Oh ! let their whiteness cover
   My hopes that paled and died.

O brother, promise-broken,
   Where drawest thou thy breath ?
Alas ! delay is token
   'Tis not delay, but death.

EGISTHUS *comes out of the palace with his sword drawn.*

EGISTHUS. -

Thy lips have said it. Be it unto thee.
Take thy farewell of all thou lookest on.

ELECTRA.

What means my lord?

ÆGISTHUS.

I mean that thou shalt die.
Now, by my sword.

ELECTRA.

O brother, brother, come!
Thou dost not mean it. Nay, thou wouldst not slay
  me.
I have no power to wrong thee. I am but
A weak and helpless girl. Let me go hence.
If I so vex thy sight, let me become
A peasant maid. Thou wilt not see me then.
Nay, do not slay me. Think upon my brother.
Haply he lives, and thou shalt live to rue
The taking of my life. Beware his wrath.

ÆGISTHUS.

Hope nothing from thy brother. He, long since,
Lay dead in Phocian soil: and thou, this day,
Here where thou standeth, shalt be laid in earth.

ÆGISTHUS *lifts his sword to slay* ELECTRA, *but, before the blow can fall,* ORESTES, *darting forward, strikes the sword out of his hand.*

ORESTES.

Twice hast thou lied, immeasurable villain!
Orestes lives, nor by thy coward hand
Shall my sweet sister die. Her children's children
Shall curse thy memory.

ELECTRA.

My father! So
I saw him yesternight. Great sir, speak to me.

ORESTES.

I'm not thy father, but thy brother, dearest.

ELECTRA.

Orestes!

ORESTES.

Not another, dear Electra.

ORESTES and ELECTRA embrace. ÆGISTHUS, recovering his sword, springs forward.

ÆGISTHUS.

The braggart fool! Now I will slay them both.

PYLADES, who has slowly entered, leaps forward and parries the blow aimed at ORESTES, when ORESTES, realizing his danger, turns upon ÆGISTHUS.

ÆGISTHUS.

What, two of you? Ho! guardmen, help! What, ho!

The guards come in.

Here, seize these strangers; bind them hand and foot.

ORESTES.

Form ye around, nor let yon wretch escape.

The guards encircle the group.

Thou seest who masters here; fool, that believed
The throne of Atreus could endure the shame

Of thy polluted form.   Behold, to-day
Thy death is, and the scattering of thy bones
To wolves and hawks.

ÆGISTHUS.

It was too long Orestes
That thou delayedst return,—for now we see
Thou art none other than thy father's son,
And king of Argive land.   How hast thou thriven
There where our forethought placed thee? For we
   feared
Some ill had met thee, it had been so long
Since news of thee came hither ; but, at last,
Thou hast returned in safety to receive
Our welcome.   Argos welcomes back with joy
Its king, into whose royal hands we yield,
With joy no less, the realm we kept for him.

ORESTES.

Woven of lies and guile, think'st thou to stay
My vengeance with sleek words? No, on this ground,
Where thy vile hand struck at my father's life,
This steel shall spill thy blood.—Prince, guard the
   girl.

ORESTES falls upon ÆGISTHUS with his sword, and they fight.   PYLADES supports ELECTRA.   For some time neither combatant prevails.   Finally ÆGISTHUS strikes ORESTES'S sword out of his hand, but, before he can follow up his advantage, PYLADES gives ORESTES his own sword, whereupon ORESTES renews the fight with redoubled fury, and soon lays ÆGISTHUS at his feet.   The guards shout.

ORESTES.

Rest thee, great Agamemnon, thou 'rt avenged!

CLYTÆMNESTRA, *hearing the uproar, comes out of the palace. She looks first at the body of her husband, and then at his victor.*

ORESTES *to* ELECTRA.

Is that my mother?

CLYTÆMNESTRA.

I am she that was,
But is no more thy mother. Let me go.
The gods but toyed with me. They let me sin,
And sin to hide my sin, and now they front me
With all my sins at once. Oh, what I was,
And what I might have been, and what I am!
Nay, slay me; end me here. Let me not live
Still to feel what I am. In pity slay me.
If ever thou didst love me, lift thy sword,
And spill my guilty life. Strike here, my son.

ORESTES.

It must not be. The gods have set thy doom
To live and know thyself for what thou art,
Till age bring thee release. Lead her away.
Drag off this carcase. Now unto the gods,
That have bestowed on us this happy hour
Will we due offering make. Best Pylades,
Friend of my heart of hearts, thou hast long since
Had all my love, and I am left too poor,
Even with love to pay thee: but thou knowest
All that I have is thine.

PYLADES.

Love asks no pay,
Else were it greed, not love. Yet, if I durst,
Thou hast one treasure I would sue thee for.

ORESTES.

'Tis thine already.

PYLADES.

Saith Electra so?

ELECTRA.

Yea, so, in sooth, my lord.

PYLADES.

Why, then, of men
Am I most happy.   Here my treasure is.

ORESTES.

It is too great an honor, noble prince.
Oh! happy day, that sees my sire avenged,
And Atreus' line restored unto its own;
That finds my sister, though but for another,
And steals my friend to give me back a brother.

THE DEATH OF GUINEVERE.

THE tale the abbess told, she that had been
The little novice, maid to Guinevere.

It was the season when there falls no night,
But all the dusk, from sun to sun, is filled
With golden twilight deepening into dawn.
Then all the air is fragrance, all the earth
Fit carpeted for foot-stool of its King
With bloom and softness. Every hour is fair,
But fairest glows the even, when the west
Uplifts its gates of pearl, and over them
The roofs and towers and spires of ruby and gold.
Then pious hearts think on the heavenly city,
And saintly eyes, wept dim o'er sins forgiven,
Now weep for rapture of the glory revealed.
But song of bird nor breath of blossom touched
With any thrill the sick heart of the queen.
Upon her bed she lay. Around, her maids
Stood weeping, while her fevered dreams outbrake:

"He loves me still, and now I go to him
To be his bride within the halls of light.
Upon their threshold he stands waiting for me,
My Arthur, king; but not as first I went
Go I to meet him in that purer world.
This time how gladly, knowing him at last!
Dreaming no more of pomp and dalliance,

But sadly, chastened with repented sin.
And purified by toil and fast and prayer,
I go to meet him who shall welcome me.
He loves me, ay! and even as at first,
When he loved only what he deemed I was,
Not what I was indeed. But now, made fair,
Save for these scars of memory, I rise
Assured of thine acceptance. O my King!

He loves me. But with earthly lips he spake.
Will he now love me in the spirit world,
Where hearts are undisguised, no beauty shines
But of the soul, nor any charm allures,
Save only purity and holiness?
Are there not myriads in the world of bliss
To be whose handmaid I were all unmeet?
Consorts he not with these, and how through them
Should I win way to him? Far other thoughts
Than memory of me must fill his soul,
Who wronged him so and served him here so ill.
He loves me; rather say he hates me not.
So at least unrebuked I may behold him.
Only to see him, this were joy enough,
My Arthur. Nay, but shall I be content
Only to see him? Was it but for this
My soul hath yearned and hoped and struggled on
These weary years? Hath he no kiss for me?
May I not clasp his knees, and in my love
Have him again all mine, my own?

       But what
If in that world the sight of me were pain,
Despite his love? As how should it not be,

Seeing that sin o'erlived is not undone,
Nor can forgiveness blot out memory?
Were sight of me to waken in his heart
Old woes, and quicken anguish of slain hopes,
Could it be love should lead me to his side?
Shall I buy joy again with pain to him?
Have I not wronged his love enough on earth,
But I must haunt him in the heavenly world,
And be his hindrance there? O Arthur, Arthur.
Must I then see thee not? May nevermore
Thy kingly glance of love sink in my heart?
I love thee, love thee! All my penitence
Hath been made light by promise of thy love;
But do I love thee so that for love's sake
I will not see thee more; that for all years
Of all eternity I can deny
Myself thy face, to spare thee sight of mine,
My love, my hope, my strength, my life, my king?
Yea for thy sake I will."

      Here ceased the queen,
And on her face a deadly pallor fell,
The light sank from her eyes;—then leaped again,
And in her cheek the rosy flush of youth
Flashed, and a smile like summer bent her lips;
She cried again "O Arthur!" and the smile
Lingered, but she had gone to meet her king.

Through the bowed window came the breath of
  morn,
And high in heaven the bright lark sang for glee.

THE GREAT ADMIRAL.

Only when leagues of sea shut out the land,
Do men discern what mountains highest stand ;
So the long years that lesser glory drown,
Reveal at last, O Farragut, thy renown !

    We knew thee bold to dare,
    We knew thee strong to do ;
  We made new honors for thee to wear,
      Till the four stars, set in blue,
        Flashed in the old-world skies
      The splendor of thine emprise.
But now how little it all appears !
    We bowed to the mighty Captain,
    But not the mightier man ;
We honored the six swift hours of crash and flame,
But not the fifty, dragging, unknown years,
    (Hard hammocks are heroes wrapped in !)
    Before the summons came,
    And Farragut's hour began.

    Now we see thee as thou wast—
      Too true to follow fame,
    And faithful at thy cost ;
So tender, thy tears would start
    At the sight of brave blood poured,
So gentle in triumph, the foeman's heart
    Was given with his sword :
Friend unfailing, pattern of men,
    As husband, father, and citizen,
Through praise and through dispraise the same.
    O mightiest toiler of the sea,

With one hand holding the waves in fee,
And the other over the mainland shut:
    Earth's greatest admiral,
      Though last yet first of all,
Yea, chief of those whom age to age shall name
Lords of the sea, De Ruyter, Nelson, Farragut!

    Some foemen to defeat
      Bringeth but little fame,
Not such the warriors it was thine to meet—
    Men bronzed in battle-flame,
And, but for the wrong they bled to save,
    The bravest of the brave.
Stout hearts in the hopeless fight,
Ye could conquer all but the right:
    How manfully ye fought!
Thunder of cannon from mound and wall,
    Earthquake shock in the river bed,
And, crackling down through all,
    The fearful fire-ships red!
    Such was the work ye wrought:
And then, after all to meet
The iron strength of your fleet—
    Grim task ye set for us!
But, if ever the day shall come—
    As we trust may never be—
    When a foe from over the sea
Shall strike at our land and home,
    Ye shall meet him even thus;
    Ye shall fight with us, side by side,
With crash of earthquake and lightning stroke,
Till the foe shall slink away in the smoke,

If he yet have strength to flee,
From defiling this hallowed shore,
That, forevermore and forevermore,
  Only the seasons shall divide,
    And a patriots' rivalry.

But, if ever in fight it should befal
That the foe, for a space, shall seem to win,
Then let his boldest hearts beware,
For, on a sudden, none knoweth from where,
A ship shall steer through the fiery din,
  That flieth the stars of the Admiral.
    —Ye shall know her by her long white deck,
      Unmarred by battle wreck;
    And in her shrouds, trumpet in hand,
    The Admiral shall stand.—
      She heeds not wave nor wind,
      She leaves no wake behind,
    No shot her hull may feel,
    But her black stem sheareth oak and steel;
And woe worth the proudest foe's renown,
On whom the Hartford beareth down.

And then, when the wars are over,
  Perchance, of a summer night,
Some pleasure-crew shall discover,
  As they lie becalmed in the light
  Of the full moon swung at height,
    A stately ship dash by,
      With open ports aglow—
    A cloud of white on the sky,
      That leaves no shadow below;
Or, haply, some fisher, blown off shore,

In the swirl of a winter storm,
Shall tell how he steered to land once more,
In the light of a ghostly form,
That sped along, full sail,
In the teeth of the winter gale,
With only a graceful heel and dip.—
It is the grand old ship,
Where Farragut, still on guard,
Keepeth perpetual watch and ward
Over the long Atlantic shore,
From granite Maine, with its deep-sea roar,
To the fragrant waves of the Gulf that he quelled of yore.

SEA AND SHORE.

Our Mother, loved of all thy sons
So dear, they die, not dying for thee;
Yet are thy fondest, tenderest ones
Thy wanderers far at sea.

Life-long the bitter blue they stem,
Till custom makes it almost fair;
Sweet grow the splintering gales to them,
The icy gloom, the scorching glare.

But thy dear eyes, which shine for all,
They see not, save through homesick tears,
Or when thy smile, through battle-pall,
Pays death and all their painful years.

Fair freedom's gospel soundeth now
    Through softer lips than those of steel;
Rust gathers on the iron prow,
    And shore weeds clog the resting keel;

To-day thou askest life, not death:
    Our lives, for life and death, are thine;
Sweet are long years, and peaceful breath,
    And sunny age beneath its vine;

But there are those that deem more fair
    (O Mother, seen at last again!)
That smile the dying see thee wear,
    Choosing thine own among the slain.

Yet, being thine, we shall be brave,
    And, being thine, we will be true;
Where'er thou callest, on field or wave,
    We wait, thy will to do.

BALDER.

Not as erst wentest thou,
    Borne on the flame-ship,—
Low thy head bentest thou,
Look nor word lentest thou
    Her on the same ship,—
Come not, thou stainless one,
    Wan to our weeping,
Come thou the painless one,
Weapon-attainless one,

Light from thee leaping.
Breidablik waits for thee,
Wide are its gates for thee,
Longeth its throne for thee,
Lie its halls lone for thee,
Loud maketh moan for thee
  Odin unsleeping.

Moonlight they needed not,
  There on that high day;
Sunlight they heeded not,
  Standing in thy day:
Glad were all hearts of thee,
Fain were all darts of thee,
  Hurled in thine honor;
Darts all were foiled of thee,
All hearts despoiled of thee,
She, still aglow for thee,
Sinketh with woe for thee,
  Death graspeth on her.

Woe's me for Balder slain,
  Valhal benighted!
Woe's me for Balder's bane,
  Mistletoe slighted!
Woe's me thy slaying hand,
  Loki, the shameless!
Woe's me, obeying hand,
  Hoder's the blameless!
Woe's me nigh sorest for
  Nanna, the blossom!
Her that thou worest for
  Joy on thy bosom.

Swift through the swaying
    Shroud of the darkness.
Who is the horseman,
    Hither that speedeth?
Wide are his wan eyes;
    Wet with sweat drops,
Hangeth his hair down,
    Hot on his brow.

He is Hermod,
    Helhome seeketh he.
Balder the Beautiful
    Bidden to save.
Sleipner bestrideth he,
    Steed of Odin;
Weeping await him,
    Wakeful, the gods.

Answer, thou speeding one,
Hasting, unheeding one,
    Back from the wonder-world,
    Spurring thy steed,
How to our eyes again,
Balder shall rise again,
    Bought from the underworld.
    What is the meed?

    Backward the blast
Beareth an answer:
    Hushed, men hear.
Hardly with breathing;
    Gold shall they give.
Glory of jewels?

What is the weird?
"Weep," answered Hermod.

Weep! thou hadst never died
    Might tears avail us:
Weep! ay, till ever dried,
    Tear-drops shall fail us!
Weep! ah, but weepeth not
    Loki the scornful;
Woe-tide he keepeth not,
    Whoso be mournful.
Hel but derideth us,
    Our tears and thy tears,
Weird now divideth us,
    Thok weepeth dry tears.

Nevermore, nevermore,
Never forevermore,
Back cometh Balder
    To Asgard again.
Niflhome foldeth him,
Blae Hel withholdeth him.
Faint grow his foot-prints
    On Breidablik's plain.

Blae Hel withholdeth him,
Niflhome foldeth him,
Asgard forgetteth him,
    Urd waxeth old.—
Lo! where supernally,
Risen eternally,
Rules he from Ragnarok
    Empires untold!

AFTERGLOW.

Jacinth, heliotrope, amethyst,
And daintier colors that have no name,
Have met and kissed in the sunset's tryst,
Till the blue sky flushes with rosy flame ;
And the darker tints the violets know
Throb in the burning afterglow,
Till suddenly, refulgent, bright,
The Star of Love leaps through the fiery gloom,
As radiant, warm and white,
As Aphrodite from the billowy bloom.

WEDLOCK.

Oh joy ! behold the earth new born,
    The former things have passed away,
And hate and malice, wrath and scorn
    Have melted in love's ray.

The life that dragged through scale and claw
    The earth-stain and the stony weight,
Leaps up an angel by love's law,
    Erect, emancipate.

And holiness no longer gleams
    A cold and distant-shining star,
But round me flash its murmuring streams,
    Its groves my covert are.

The birds are singing "Love, love, love!"
    For love the warm sun shines on high,
And in my heart a bliss above
    The noonday light makes melody.

Sweet wife, mine own, mine, only mine,
    Long sought, at last all, all mine own,
In reverence our lives combine,
    And mount on honor as a throne.

IN THE KINGDOM OF THE BLIND THE ONE-EYED IS KING.

In the Kingdom of the Blind,
Softness, harmony I find,
Fragrance, flavors ne'er excelled,—
All that pleases unbeheld.
But the people have no eyes,
And they hear with wild surprise,
With a measureless delight,
When I speak to them of sight,
Press to learn the wondrous thing,
Clasp me, crown me, hail me king;

Me! that in the Land of Seeing,
Have but half a scanty being,
Am despised and scorned of men,—
But in Blindman's-Land, ah! then,
You should hear of my renown,
You should see my robe and crown!

Impromptu, 28th Sept., 1884.

POETS.

CREATURES of the kind that browse
The yet unwithered Eden boughs;
All qualities in them unite,
"The quintessence of every sprite,"
Dantean groans, Homeric laughter;
Eye-witnesses of all the past,
They hold the present's rapture fast,
Contemporaries of the hereafter.

CHAMPLAIN GLIMPSES.

WHERE the brimmed sky hath spilt itself between
   The parted Emerald and Empire states,
A wavering line, from Horicon, the sheen,
   To where the lake-devouring Lawrence waits
For sweet Champlain, which still smiles on serene,
   Now stretching broad, now cramped by frowning
      straits,
Now nestling to uplift a cup of blue,
Distilled of pines' and harebells' honey-dew;

And on this deep-blue, lower heaven rest
   Sweet island stars, nor want there cloudlets white
To lure the eye, whether they lie caressed
   By the smooth flood, or whether, with swift flight,
They speed above the water's fluttered breast,
   Or whether, dimly outlined in the night,
They glide like ghosts by cliff and curving shore,
And charm the ear with song when seen no more.

If beauty be thy quest, then look around.
    Wears earth a smile more radiant than this?
These rocky, jutting headlands, forest-crowned,
    These low, broad meadows leaning down to kiss
The violet flood ; these island crags fast bound,
    These vistas where the eyes in wonder miss
The old embrace of wooded shore and sky.
To find the watery blue clasp that on high.

BARRED OUT.

OUT of the schools, into the light of God.
From dungeon walls to fields where Shakespeare trod ;
Out of the churches into holiness,
Where priest-spurned Milton felt God's presence bless ;
Out of society, which frets and mars.
To solitude with earth and sea and stars ;
Banished from sloth and pride and discontent.
O Heart, how easy is thy banishment !

ICARUS.

'Tis something, from that tangle to have won ;
'Tis something to have matched the wild-bird's flight ;
'Tis something to have soared and touched the sun.
What, though the lashing billows roar beneath?
Better than death in life is life in death :—
    Good night !

THE QUESTION.

Who is the more to blame,
    The woman or the man?
    Now tell me ye that can;
Or is their guilt the same,
And have they equal shame,
    One sin and ban?

If he the tempter played,
    Was she not tempter too,
    Though most when least she knew?
And was not woman made
Harder to be assayed,
    Though weaker once untrue?

Let God their guilt allot,
    Who made them man and woman.
    (Who made shall not undo man!)
The worst are bad, God wot,
The best not without spot,
    And all are human.

Impromptu, 29th Dec., 1883.

BLINDNESS.

Not only "with souls that cringe and plot,
We Sinais climb and know it not;"
Life-long we walk through Canaan's land,
Unweeting but of desert sand.

THE BURDEN.

To make life lovelier and Heaven nearer,
Truth more delightful, and its pathway clearer,
And holiness more attainable and dearer ;

Teaching that beauty is no more nor less
Than the eternal radiance of holiness,
And never vice clad in a brighter dress :

That love and lust are mutual foes that slay,
Love from Heaven a world-enlightening ray,
And lust a smothering smoke of Hell-birth aye :

That only one truth means all lies but one,
That all truth often means not all but none,
That truth and lies oft in one thread are spun :

The blackest pool will show an angel's face,
If but an angel shadow it ; such grace
Hath holiness, such hidden good the base ;—

For song is when the poet's heart o'erflows,
Far lie its springs ; thou seest nor rains nor snows,
Nor the dark ways that crystal water goes.

ST. ELIZABETH.*

Fair maid, whom silken robes adorn
   Less than thy purity and grace,
What shadow, on thy bridal morn,
   Is this that falls upon thy face?

---

*The last painting by Miss Eliza Austin. St. Elizabeth of Hungary is represented as a young and beautiful girl in bridal array, standing with down-cast eyes. The pose of the figure is inexpressibly sweet and maidenly. I was honored by the assurance of the lamented artist that I had correctly interpreted in my lines the thoughts of the "dear saint."

Is joy to sorrow so akin
  That love must bring thee downcast eyes,
And present raptures only win
  Thy soul to banished miseries?

Delayest thou, whose head so long
  Was bowed in sorrow as in night,
To lift thine eyes, lest, rayed too strong,
  Fond Love should blind thee with its light?

Or is thy dread that earthly bliss
  And sweets of human love may lure
Thy soul from Him whose own it is,
  Who died to make thy life secure?

But fear not, sweet Elizabeth,
  Thy feet are in the heavenly way;
Thou shalt not lose, in life or death,
  His hand to lead, His arm to stay.

The Master still hath need of thee,
  On this dark earth a light to shine;—
So shalt thou live, and thus shall be
  That early going-forth of thine;

As when, o'er purple heights of snow,
  Descends the hastening winter sun,
Leading men's eyes aloft, and lo!
  The shining host, whereof 'tis one.

25th July, 1886.

COUSIN NELL.

WE have thee still.   Life had to fame revealed thee ;
    Pain kept thee ours alone ;
And death, releasing thee from pain, hath sealed thee
    Immortally our own.

Thou seest now, with angel vision clearer,
    The sweet home-world we see,
And the fair heavens have fairer grown and dearer,
    Beheld again by thee.

Ay, and above the orbs of His creation,
    Thou seest the Ineffable ;
Thy lips take up the anthemed adoration
    That seraph voices swell.

There doubts no more the hunted spirit capture,
    Nor any pains annoy ;
No tears are there, or only tears of rapture.
    No burden but of joy.

Oh, earthly dream !   What knew the clod of seeing,
    Or wist of nature's plan,
Before God breathed on it, and thrilled with being,
    The dust leaped up a man ?

15th Nov., 1885.

ESTRANGED.

Light on the lake,
  And mirth on the lea,
Rest and gladness
  To thee and me;

Gray wings glancing
  Athwart the sky,
Music swelling
  Through tree-tops high;

White sails bending
  With flash or gloom,
Fragrance outbreathing
  From leaf and bloom;

The half-seen veil
  O'er the sky hovering,—
Was it cloud or smoke,
  Or an angel's wing?

Oh! joys that fled,
  To come not again!
Oh! hope and longing,
  Which left but pain!

FATED.

"Come up," he said, "the walls are low,
 Pluck heart, and lightly leap them o'er."
Alas! the walls of Heaven bow
 Before the chosen and no more.

THE SEASONS.

When winter skies are polished green,
And pine trees tall with snow-drifts lean,
And black brooks gurgle out of sight,
Beneath the dimpled snow-crust white,
And birchen underwoods do dress
In lace-work of their leaflessness;
Oh! then, methinks, of all the year,
The windy winter is most dear.

When spring has on the willows lighted,
And redder combs the cocks have dighted,
And through the lingering twilight's gold,
The swollen brooks roar manifold,
And, day by day, the pastures gray
Grow green in spite of flocks that stray;
'Tis then, of all the full year brings,
I deem the richest gifts the spring's.

The hovering skies are soft and blue,
Which massy, white clouds, loitering through,
Trail mile-wide shadows as they pass,
Above the green and springing grass:
The shielding elms are wide and strong,
The maples dusky grots of song,—
The high tide of the heart and year,
The scented summer time is here.

What thing is likest unto fall?
The rainbow's banded coronal,
Cathedral windows bright and high,
The glories of the sunset sky,

The splendor told of tropic birds,
Rapture of music, woven words
That bind the spell of poesy,—
All these, and all that fairest be, .
Reveal thy absence, but not thee!

ISLE AU HAUT.

Highland island of the deep,
   Isle au Haut !
Where the storm-winds wailing sweep,
And the breakers flash and leap.
   All a-row,
Echoing up thy rocky steep,
   Isle au Haut.

Thee we watch from far away,
   Isle au Haut,
Giant guardian of the bay,
Bidding ocean's onset stay,
   Heedless, though
Deep thy woods are drenched with spray,
   Isle au Haut.

Utmost outpost of the land,
   Isle au Haut,
Mountain-walled on every hand,
With thy frothed and broken strand,
   White as snow,
And thy lake the fairies planned,
   Isle au Haut.

Miles away I see thee shine,
  Isle au Haut,
Sunset on those cliffs of thine,
Rosy-flushed thy darkling pine,
  While, below,
Ship-lights glimmer on the brine,
  Isle au Haut!

DAY-RED.

Light, and the fading of night;
 Light and the glory of dawn;
Life the indwelling of light,
 And death when the light is withdrawn!

A glory that feeling can see,
 A glory that seeing can feel;
A gleam of the glory to be,
 That earth cannot wholly conceal.

Light, and the fleeing of night,
 Light and the onset of day;—
But the dark flees not always with light,
 Nor waits for the night-time alway.

REST.

The head-drawn arrow sleeping on the string;
The sky-wrapt eagle hung on level wing.

CHILD OF THE NORTHERN STAR.

Child of the Northern Star,
   Rocked on the deep sea's breast,
Earth calleth from afar,
   Leave now thy nest!
Come from thy cliff-built home,
Out of its frost and foam,
   Child of the Northern Star
   Like storm-bird, come!

Seest thou the splintered light,
   Shot through the northern sky?—
Leaping of sword-blades bright,
   In Valhal high.
There sit thy fathers old,
After toils manifold :
   Child of the Northern Star,
   Be thou as bold!

Let winter's blight of doom
   Bury earth from foot and eye,
Let winter's awful bloom
   Blaze in the sky :
Then let the summer's glee
Glimmer on land and sea :
   Child of the Northern Star,
   'Tis not for thee!

Thy path to southward lies,
   Unto the lands of the sun,
Where stricken Freedom cries,
   Heeded by none.

    Hence, haste to help her, go,
    Smite down her dastard foe,
      Child of the Northern Star,
      Help! Southward, ho!

NOT THE SAME.

Not the same, oh! not the same,
    Mounts the brightening sun at morn:
Not the same, nor yet the same,
    Dips the moon her golden horn.
Sweet the morning light may be,
Silver sweet on land and sea.
    Fair the moon on wave and shore,
    Fair and golden as before,
Sweet and fair, but changed to me,
    Seeing thee, alas! no more.

Not the same, though sweet and fair,
    Sweet and fair, but not the same;
For a sadness everywhere
    Broods with whisperings of thy name:
Veils the risen morning's light,
Deepens with the deepening night.
    Mourns thee on the murmuring strand,
    Sways about me as I stand,
In a world with summer bright,
    Seeing gloom on every hand.

UNHIDDEN.

O BILLOWY Pines afar,
    That belt with purple the sea,
Do you think with your boughs to bar
    The infinite ocean from me?

I see in the wavy line,
    That you pencil on the sky,
The sweep that the swaying brine
    Takes on when the wind is high;

The beautiful, shifting blue,
    That silkenly veils you alway,
Is only the ocean's hue,
    Which, hiding, you betray;

And I know that, if I came nigh,
    Your own would reveal to me
The ocean's tremulous sigh,
    And its perfume wafted free!

AUTUMN.

GOLDEN and russet and golden,
    Low-lying, lustrous, and still;
As fair as the garden of olden,
    That Adam was given to till!

Scarlet and purple and scarlet,
    Emerald, amber, and pearl;
As brilliant as sunset afar-lit,
    And soft as a singing shell's whorl!

Autumn, the queen of the seasons!
Thou scatterest beauty like rain.
And, lo! here we give thee allegiance,
And, vassals, fall into thy train!

LOVE'S FALTERING.

With bright prow parting the waters wan,
    Love sailed from shore in the morning gray,
His white sails taut with the damps of dawn,
    His white decks spattered with spurting spray,
His banners blowing above the mist,
    And flushed with a faint fore-feeling glow
Of the rosy warmth in the reddening east,
    From the sun of his yearning so far below.

And ever the wake span out astern
    Its thread that whitened and frayed away,
And ever the banners did brightlier burn,
    And the mists waxed thinner and rosier aye:
And Love leaped laughing to see how fast
    The far shore sank, and laughed to behold
The red light glinting above the mast,
    And the low clouds blazing purple and gold.

And ever crisping and curling spring
    Twin sheaves of white athwart the prow,
That, lifting ever and shattering, fling
    Their foam-fruit over the decks of snow.

The sky is throbbing with white and red,
   And gilded is every green wave's crest,
But Love looks back and sees with dread
   The low shore sunk in the kindling west.

The shore hath sunk in the kindling west,
   But still the sunlight is not yet,
And, strangely chilling on cheek and breast,
   The breezes come from the land that is set ;
And, strangely blinding, out of the dawn
   A thousand blazing splendors leap.
And Love, with pallid lips withdrawn,
   Sails fearfully down that blossoming deep.

O happy Love, thou art all alone,
   Thou art sailing alone on a wide, white sea,
And the sunlight's warmth is about thee thrown,
   And the sunlight's beauty is over thee.

THE POET AND THE BIRDS.

Sing no more of light on the snow,
   From the faint and southward-shrunken sun ;
No more of winds that forget to blow,
   For a space, when the shivering day is done ;
Sing of the songless winter no more,
For the birds are piping at every door.

They sing of a summer that is to be,
    And a winterless, aye-bright summer afar,
Which they, in their kindness, have left that we
    Might hearken and learn what its beauties are.
Liegemen of Summer, children of Light,
How fondly the warm Sun follows your flight!

And the children hear them, and throng to the pane,
    Pale faces glad that summer is nigh;
The poet hears them, and murmurs, "Again
    I yield unto one that is greater than I.
What need have men of an earthly song,
When Heaven sings to them the whole day long?

I sang in the darkness and cold to men
    Warm songs of hope from a heart that was chill:
And all took courage that heard me then
    But praised me never, or singing or still;
And here in the warmth, when the winter is done,
There's that in my bosom that knows not the sun.

O poets of summer, sing now while ye may,
    And gladden the earth with your music and light:
There yet must be winter, and who shall dare say,
    But, when ye have left us to cold and the night,
That somewhere then in the darkness may be
Some heart that will fain hear a song from me?"

A BLUSH.

Her cheek, which with the white rose strove and won,
Was by the red rose color overdone.

MY CHILD-LOVE.

The sun was in the sky,
    The blue was bright above,
When up the river I
    Went sailing to my love;
The bonny, wee lassie that loveth me,
The one sweet lassie I fain would see.

As on and up we sped,
    And upward still and on,
The sunset fired and fled,
    Then fired, and then was gone;
The splendor faded into gray,
And white mists gathered along our way.

But high above the west,
    There burst a splendid star,
The star of all the best
    To those that loving are;
And away in the darkling depths I knew
The eyes that I love beheld it too.

I see the star to-night,
    It burneth still above.
But not the morrow's light
    Shall bring me to my love;
Yet the two blue eyes that still I see,
I wonder if now they watch for me.

And oh! whene'er again
    I sail my love to meet.
God grant I find her then
    As innocent and sweet.
As when her last kiss robbed my heart
Of all but its longing and aching part.

PRINCESS EYEBRIGHT.

Princess Eyebright's seventeen,
No more princess but a queen.
Who would ever guess 'twas she
Used to sit upon my knee,
Bid we tell of sleeping Rip,
Culprit Fay and flying ship,
Or, from old-world bring her back
Puss-in-boots and climbing Jack :
Then, when I had said my say,
Pouted her bright lips for pay?
Though she's grown since then, somehow
Her lips are farther from me now.
Yet she lifts in olden wise
Dusky veiled, violet eyes ;
But the look they wear is new,
Shy, and yet so trustful too,
That I swear the girl I miss
Charmed me never so as this.

CRITICISM.

With what measure ye mete ye do therewith
Measure unto yourselves; and whosoever
Judgeth another, in that selfsame act,
Is by himself condemned ; for criticism
Is a two-edged blade without a handle,
Whose sharpest blows wound sorest him that wields.

BOOT AND SADDLE.

Boot and saddle,
    To horse and away!
Up with the dawn,
    And on with the day!
Hark! afar-off
    Rattles the fray;
Boot and saddle,
    To horse and away!

Up, where the hard flints
    Flash as we fly,
On, where the hot dust
    Rolls to the sky;
Death flash, death-cloud
    Wait us to-day;
Boot and saddle,
    To horse and away!

Loud and louder
    The battle blast calls,
Haste and hurl you,
    Where innocence falls:
Shame on the coward
    Would falter and stay,
When, comrades, hurrah!
    We are up and away.

GRANT.

Last of the Mighty Three,
Upholders of liberty,
Now art thou once more
With the great that have gone before,—
Lincoln, anguish-eyed,
Struck down mid a world's acclaim,
And loyal Farragut, who died
Unscathed by bolt or flame.
Last of the mighty, thou;
And the nations in mourning bow,
With the foemen of long ago,
At thy first, last overthrow;
While the land thou hast left secure
Sits widowed, lone and poor,
With only that empty pall
In place of Our General.

1st August, 1885.

ÇA IRA.

Haste not, halt not; it will go:
Truth cannot be hindered so.
Without pain was never birth.
Drops the seed in April earth,
And above it, fierce and white,
Suns of summer blasting smite.
Waves the brown September mead,
Gleams the corn where fell the seed.
They alone, 'twas ever so,
Overcome, that undergo.

Flinch not, faint not; time will tell;
Heaven keeps its reckoning well.
Into childhood's laughing eyes
Rush the tears of toil's surprise.
Striving on from sun to sun,
Nothing ever find we done.
Toil of hand and toil of brain,
Task and toil, but all in vain;
Faileth heart and fadeth hope,
As the shadows eastward slope.
Last the uproar dies away:
Then like music: "Only they
(God in wisdom willed it so),
Overcome, that undergo!"

THE EARTH-SCHOOL.

God giveth seasons, change of moon,
Gloaming and midnight, dawn and noon,—
With ruddy youth and rheumy eld,
And joy by sorrow still dispelled,
And love and all that love can bring,
And hate, with all its following,
And death's curst robberies,—lest we,
Secure in immortality,
Should slight those lessons, which alone
Make immortality our own.

SELF-DECEPTION.

O LOVER, it is not she thou lovest,
   The maiden that hears thee with scared surprise,
Not she, but thine ideal of woman,
   Whereon thou never hast laid thine eyes.

And more, O lover, I'll tell thee a secret,
   Which tortures could not make thee confess,
That even now, in the midst of thy pleading,
   Thou 'dst rather she'd say thee no than yes.

DAVID BARKER.

THE babbling brooks repeat his name,
The weird pines whisper of his fame,
His spirit broods o'er the sweet lake's rest,
His grander presence lifts the mountain's crest,
While the round heavens that meet the bluer hills
Guard lovingly the land his memory fills.

Katahdin Iron Works, 11th August, 1884.

THE DIFFERENCE.

TO M. L. W.

How pleasant in the crowd to meet
A face so fair, a look so sweet,
A form so fine, where every grace
Has fixed its lightsome dwelling place!

"Yes, and how much she looks like May!"
Alas! with gold compare not clay.
In yonder maiden now I see
Not beauty but deformity.

MATERIALISM.

Tell me, was not this the guilt
Of those that Babel's column built?

They sought by outward height to rise
To the heaven that in man lies;

So in wrath God changed their speech,
Each builder babbling unto each,

Vainly as those that strive to-day
To reach the soul o'er steps of clay.

LEFT BEHIND.

(The poet speaks.)

I sit upon the rooted wharf,
    And watch the ships away.
Some go in shine, and some in shower,
    And all to leave the bay;
But, shower or shine, no ship is mine,
    Look wheresoe'er I may.

Some are but skiffs that hug the strand,
    Some larger, coast-wise bound,
While some are mighty ships that go,
    To sail the great world round.
Some carry peace, with earth's increase,
    And some war's thunder sound.

Upon their lessening decks I see
    My boyhood's fellows stand.
But yesterday I spake with them
    Of many a far-off land,
And of the sea, and how, ah me!
    Our keels should spurn the strand.

Now all are gone, and here I sit,
    Upon the lonely shore,
While others, younger, pass me by,
    And go as those before,
Till all unknown, I sit alone,
    And look the waters o'er.

Sometimes the landward breezes bring
    Brave tidings from afar,
Of battles won, and victories
    Not less than those of war,
Of golden sands in shining lands,
    That far to southward are.

Sometimes the sea-fared ships come back,
    Laden with outland spoil,
With gold and silk, with furs for which
    The buskined hunters toil,
Coral and shells from Indian dells,
    And sandal, wine and oil.

Then too sometimes drift landward slow,
    Sea-bleached with living mail,
A splintered plank, a broken spar,
    That tell a sadder tale
Of those that sleep beneath the deep,
    Unheeding wave or gale.

And then I think and ask myself
    If it were not more sweet,
To lie as these do, in their cold
    And watery winding-sheet,
Than not to know how storm-winds blow,
    And how the great waves beat.

But still I trust that God, who gave
    The broad sea unto man,
Knows what is best, and wills that I
    Should serve Him all I can ;
So, haply, He but orders me
    To hinder not His plan.

O faint-heart, thus to sit and sigh,
    For what no sighing brings !
What boots it that thou art not sent
    On seaward wanderings ?
Hath not the air bright paths to fare,
    And thou, hast thou not wings ?

SOUL AND BODY.

Enough to keep soul and body together ;
Enough to keep them apart, say rather.

OUT OF THE DEPTHS.

They fable how, what time the star
Led on to Bethlehem from afar,
That by the islands of the west,
A sailor, seeking port and rest,
With homesick prow unwillingly
Frothing the wine of the cloud-lit sea,
Heard through the dusk a voice that said,
Loud from the shore: "Great Pan is dead."
The frightened sailor told his tale;
Some stopped to listen, some turned to rail.
Speaker and speech have passed away,
But who believes in Pan to-day?

I trod the black-walled city through.
Wherein no man his brother knew.
But every one went hurrying by,
Seeking his own with foot and eye.
The ground was frozen, dry and bare,
A hint of snow was in the air;
When, suddenly, the city's roar,
That rang from railway and street and store,
Till it rose with the streaming smoke on high,
And smote against the shutting sky,
Came echoed back from overhead
In words that thundered: "God is dead!"

I wonder I did not shriek with fear,
But no man seemed to heed or hear,
So with a shudder I hurried on,
And what I had heard I told to none.
For is it not better that men should live,
Caring naught for the naught they give.

Believing in beauty and truth and love,
Than to know there is nothing below or above?
For how is falsehood worse than truth,
Or love than hate, or wreak than ruth,
And where shall beauty now abide,
When God, who made man's heart, has died?

Religion is a pleasing cheat,
Then let us hug the fair deceit.
God is dead; the heavens are brass,
And life is brittle as last year's grass.
Still in the sky the stars run on,
But only as wheels when the power is gone,
Or as wisdom dwells in an old man's brain,
When his manhood's thoughts rise up again.

They tell us man was made for truth :
But truth or falsehood, now, forsooth,
We'll take whichever suits us best,
Since each man's God is in each man's breast.
So much of godhead liveth still,
That good is the good and the ill is ill ;
But so much only ; wrong and right
With God are buried and out of sight,
And the ugly ought is put to sleep ;
Pleasure's commandments alone we'll keep.

But if this be and go untold,
While saints bear crosses for crowns of gold,
I ought to tell them they trust a lie,
That they may be merry before they die.
I ought.—ah me, the word I said !
The God of Sinai is then not dead :

It must have been the Christ that died,
And I think I know what pierced his side.
These were the weapons that laid him low:
The hand of his friend and the heart of his foe.

Sin!—He thought to bear alone
The burden that made the whole world groan.
He has lifted and shouldered the mighty load,
But can he bear it the lone, long road?
Neglect from his own; ah, that was the thing
That broke that heart of suffering!
And all mankind must forever die,
Because of the church's perfidy.
Worse off are we than the men of yore,
With God above and no Christ before.

So railed I, bitter in heart and word,
As if it were truth that I had heard,
Nor ever guessed that the voice had been
Only an echo of human sin.
But straightway a whisper low replied:
" The risen Christ no more hath died;
And, though he be wounded again and again,
Christ beareth the burden of sin amain."
I looked, and saw, in the drifting dust,
Two starving children snatch at a crust,
And the stronger yield it with fleshless hand,
Then straightway sink on the freezing sand.
A blush of shame spread over my brow,
As the still small voice made answer now:
" Wherever self-hating love shall abide,
Stands in her beauty the Church, the Bride."

I turned, and lo ! the children were gone.
Was it a vision I looked upon ?
I never knew, but this I ken,
That Christ the Helper walked with me then.

A SUMMER NIGHT IN WINTER.

Lulled is every breath of breeze,
   Low hath sunk the evening star,
Down behind the western trees,
   Dim the other planets are :

High and proudly rides the Moon,
   Noon renewing with her light,
In her train I read the rune,
   That the sister Pleiads write.

All around, the voiceful pines
   Hush their whispers and adore.
Low the distant sea reclines,
   And its deeps forget their roar.

But for missing its perfume,
   I could think the hour were May :
Never spring, with all its bloom,
   Did a fairer night display.

Would our lives were ordered so,
   Spring at heart throughout the year,
Winter-lit with summer's glow,
   Till the newer spring appear !

THE NORNS.

A VISION of the northern sisters weird,
Whom, in the days of eld, our fathers worshipped,
Verdande, Urd and Skuld, the Present, Past
And Future; for methought I heard them sing,
Standing upon a windy hill-top hoar
Of bygone years; mayhap upon that day,
When Olaf, bringer of the gospel, died
In sea-fight with the worshippers of Thor,
Or most believed he died; so, hand in hand,
Their golden locks broad-blowing over brows
That mocked the morning, sang the maiden Fates.

Born while time was not,
    Always and ever the same,
Daughters of that high God,
    Whom gods nor men may name,
The God who sitteth aloft,
    Fearless of storm and shock,
By whom are given, Earth, Hell and Heaven,
    Unto us till the Ragnarok.
The lives of gods and men,
    And laughter and toil and tears,
The shadowy yearnings of youth
    And the darkness that comes with years,
The skill of the hand that shapes,
    The craft of the mind that plans,
The might of love that blesses
    The strength of hate that bans.
The wrath of men that strive,
    And blood, and the madness of fight,

    The hiss of the sword that cleaves,
        The scream of arrows that smite,—
    All this, to make or mangle,
        Doth God upon us bestow,
    The while we twine for the kingdoms nine,
        The threads of mirth and woe.

The younger two here paused; the Past went on:
    The things that were and are not,
        And never more shall be,
    Are not and shall be never,
        By will and word of me.
    Under the tree Ygdrasil,
        The god-upholding ash,
    Beneath the root that leads to heaven,
        My well-spring's waters flash;
    And, from those leaping waters,
        My sisters, every day,
    With me anew its leaves bedew,
        That it may bloom for aye;
    And hither, on the rainbow,
        The ten gods, riding, come,
    And hither Thor, through the rivers four,
        Wades to the mote of doom:
    But hither comes not Balder,
        He must in Helhome bide,
    Till heaven and earth, from the new birth,
        Awaken purified.
    So never cometh Balder,
        And never comes again
    The good that was aforetime,
        To gods or vans or men;

> But neither shall be ever
>   The evil once gone by,
> For so I will, and warder
>   Of all the past am I.
> Mine are the deeds of all men,
>   And all, men think or say,
> I hold it unforgotten,
>   Until the dooming day.
> I stand by every cradle,
>   With fear and longing rife,
> What time I lay in gold or gray,
>   The warp for the web of life.

No sooner ceased the Past than, looking up,
With eyes of noonday blue, the Present sang:

> Mine is the time that is,
>   The high-tide of to-day,
> The fleeting now that hastens,
>   And yet abides for aye.
> I stand by every birth-bed,
>   And lay the twisted woof
> That binds the web of being
>   For bale or for behoof.
> I stood by the great Father,
>   When, out of the unseen,
> He shaped the fire-and mist-worlds,
>   And the Yawning-gap between.
> I saw the spring Hvergelmer
>   In the midst of Niflhome,
> And the twelve streams, Elivagar,
>   That ice-cold flowed therefrom;

I saw the giant Ymer
    Shaped from the drifted steam ;
I saw the cow Audhumbla
    That fed along the stream.
The sons of Bor beheld I,
    The sons that Bestla nursed.
Vile and Ve and Odin,
    Odin of gods the first ;
I saw the giant Ymer
    Slain by the children three,
I saw Bergelmer's household
    Float on the bloody sea,
And then the new earth shapen
    From Ymer's flesh and bone,
And over it the giant's skull,
    To form the heaven thrown ;
I saw the sparks from Muspelhome,
    Each, rising, form a star ;
I saw the shining Sun-maid
    Drawn in her shielded car ;
And when Earth bred the dwarf-kind,
    It passed within my ken,
And when the high gods gave them
    The shape and mind of men.
But still mankind I saw not,
    Until the sons of Bor,
Finding the twain trees lifeless,
    That stood upon the shore,
Made from them Ask and Embla,
    The eldest human pair,
And gave them life and motion,
    And mind and features fair.

And so all things that have been
    I saw, and so I see
All things that are, and shall see
    All things that are to be.
Hereat the Future took the mystic song,
And, looking far away, far-speaking, sang:

The past is forever no more,
    And what is the present but past?
The future abideth for aye,
    The youngest, the newest, the last.
My sisters may mete out and spin
    Their web at the birth-tides of men,
That weird-cloth my fingers shall rend.
    As ever, forever again.
For I order all that shall be,
    From Nidhug to Gimle the bright:
The secrets of storm-cloud and tears,
    The secrets of laughter and light,
The secrets of dying and birth,
    The secrets of all things to come,
And, latest and greatest of all,
    The Ragnarok's god-quelling gloom.
For earth shall wax older and worse,
    And a lie shall be sweeter than truth,
And there shall be strife, and the spilling of life,
    And dead shall be mildness and truth;
So onward, till come three winters,
    When the sun shall yield no mirth,
And sleet and snow shall fall
    From the corners of the earth;

Three winters without a summer,
    And then come other three,
When war and wrath shall redden
    The earth from sea to sea.
Then shall the Fenris-wolf
    Break loose and swallow the sun,
The moon shall Moongarm swallow,
    The stars shall shatter down.
The Midgard-circling serpent
    Shall writhe and reach the land,
And by his side the Fenrer
    Shall take his fiery stand;
And hither Hrym the foe-fiend
    Shall on the Nail-ship steer,
The ship that now is building,
    Through every thoughtless year.
Then shall the sky be cloven,
    And, down the shining way,
The glittering sons of Muspel
    Shall ride in long array.
The rainbow, no more needed,
    Shall break beneath their feet,
As into Vigrid's field they wend,
    The Asgard ranks to meet.
Meanwhile ariseth Heimdal,
    And winds the Gjallar horn,
Which bids the blithe gods hie them
    Into the fight forlorn.
At the wild blast Ygdrasil
    Shivers in root and trunk;
Then feels the fount of Mimer
    Its waters strangely sunk;

While all the Valhal heroes,
    With gladsome hearts and high,
Speed onward fast, to the trumpet blast,
    Where Odin leads to die.
Then against fell Fenrer
    Shall Odin lift the spear;
Then, at the foul serpent,
    Shall Thor his Mjolner rear;
Then Surt, the Muspel-warder,
    Shall spill the heart of Frey,
Who bitterly shall rue him
    The blade he gave away.
Meanwhile the Midgard-serpent
    Lies dead upon the ground,
Beside him Thor, his victor,
    Lieth in venom drowned.
The wolf hath swallowed Odin.
    But Vidar, fearing naught,
Lifting the welded shoe,
    Throughout the ages wrought,
Shall tread the fiend-wolf's jaw,
    And, straining hand and head,
Shall tear and rend until he lay
    His father's conqueror dead.
Then Loke slayeth Heimdal,
    And slain himself shall fall,
Then Surt, the Frey-destroyer,
    Warder of Muspelhal,
Shall rise, and through the wan earth
    Far scatter fire and low,
Till the great tree Ygdrasil
    Shall vanish in the glow;

Till, crashing to its embers,
    Shall fall that earth-old tree,
And all the world, in smoke-wreaths whirled,
    Shall sink beneath the sea.
But, though o'er the nine kingdoms,
    That starless dusk shall set,
And earth and sky be vanished,
    The end shall not be yet.
For lo! as in the Northland,
    The lingering summer sun
Drops in the sea at midnight,
    And, sunken, mounts anon,
While all the gathering darkness
    Gives way to morning's light,
So, from the gloom, a new earth
    Upspringeth fresh and bright.
For now the great Allfather
    Hath judged the things of yore,
And all the good comes back again
    To last forevermore.
So, on the new earth's meadows,
    Vidar and Vale stand;
Before them goeth Magne,
    The Mjolner in his hand;
Beside him walketh Mode,
    And, lo! apart from all,
In silence Hœner sitteth,
    Watching what may befal;
And see, by Hoder standing,
    The Balder of the past,
For, drowned in ocean, all things
    Have wept for him at last.

> The fair Sun's fairer daughter
>   Rides through the gladdened sky,
> And lights a race of sinless men
>   That neither weep nor die.

So sang the Future; and her elders twain,
With lifted hands, joined with her in a cry
That thrilled me long after their words had ceased:

> Man is a breath in the cold,
>   A shadow that wrinkles the ground.
> He cometh and goeth, and lo!
>   His footsteps can nowhere be found.
> He climbeth the walls of the sky,
>   But he cannot arise from the sod;
> He toileth; the toil is his own,
>   The end of his work is with God!

LAPLAND DRIVING-SONG.

SPRING, my reindeer fleet,
On with bounding feet!
　Over ice and snow,
　Swift, my swift one go!
What care we for cold—
　Cold or driving storm?
　Though the house be warm,
Snug the mossy fold,
Naught but star and snow-hung tree
Shall our light and shelter be.

In the winter night,
   While moons wax and wane,
   Rise and sink again,
And no sun gives light;
   While the flaming north
   Flaunts its banners forth,
Then we hunt the seal,
Armed with rope and steel,
Scouring floe and frozen fiord,
For the hunter's prized reward.

Now, my reindeer swift,
Speed above the drift,
   Skim the river-bed,
   While right overhead,
Hangs the northern star,
   With the sleepless Bear
   Circling in the air,
Watching it afar.
Snow beneath and stars above,
Winter is the time we love!

THE SMALL TO THE GREAT.

NAY, scorn us not, ye poets throned for aye,
Us painful singers of a fleeting day.
We have our worth: we din the world's dull ear
With song until men cannot choose but hear;
Yet, forced to listen, heed they you, not us.
And so our low fame lifts your glorious.

CAMDEN HILLS.

Oh! Camden Hills are fair to sea,
    Over the misty bay,
When the breakers lighten under the lee,
And the waves like liquid iron be,
Whereon the raindrops fitfully
    Whiten and sink away.

And Camden Hills are grand to view
    Under the morning's eye,
When the feathery clouds are high and few,
And the hills have caught the heaven's own blue,
And the waves are bright with the selfsame hue
    Of the mountains and the sky.

But, oh! most lovely to behold
    Are Camden Hills, to me,
When the sunset mantles the west with gold,
And the pearly vapors manifold
Are slowly up to the mountains rolled,
    Over the rainbow sea.

HEREDITY.

We chose not what we are, nor can unmake
More than we could have made. How strange it
    seems!
One, bowed to earth, sees but the sticks, the rake,
And one, in Beulah dwelling, sings in dreams.

THE FROZEN WATERFALL.

HEADLONG over the headland's brow,
   When skies were soft and winds blew west,
Thy diving waters dashed, which now
      Rest.

For a wind came out of the wintry north,
   And the roar of waters that shook the hill,
Suddenly stricken, grew thenceforth
      Still.

The pillar of white, which the light wind swayed,
   Bends not now in any blast;
For its waters hang, in mid-leap stayed
      Fast.

Marble torrent! a rest how deep!
   Yet rest, not death, is thine, for anon
Thy loosened waters shall dash with a leap
      On.

EDWIN BOOTH.

LET Shakespeare hold the mirror up to nature,
Show scorn her image, virtue her own feature;
'Tis not enough without thy glorious part
To hold the mirror up to Shakespeare's art.

EBEEME.

Bright is the broad Ebeeme as in the days gone by ;
So little Nature sorrows when those that love her die.
The vast pine's benediction still greets the wakening
    year,
Still from the snow-bank's edges the pink-white May-
    blooms peer,
With bowstring-twang the wild-fowl bend here their
    arrow-flight,
What time the full-moon lingers below the floor of
    night,
And long before the swart snow has left the shadiest
    glen,
The winter-starven partridge drums merrily again.

There is no southern hillside but coins itself in gold,
And every violet's fingers their fill of heaven hold ;
Here, as in Junes aforetime, the shy, red strawberries,
    strawn,
Blush to the water's redness that eyes the early dawn ;
And when the flowers of springtime have breathed
    their light away,
And August's blackened clover no more perfumes the
    day,
Still flash the scarlet cardinals along Ebeeme's shore,
Like elfin bale-fires mourning the blooms that are no
    more.
Upon its heaving shallows the anchored lilies nod,
Greeting the purple asters and plumy golden-rod ;

Hushed are the summer's voices, its uproar and its
    song,

All but the picket challenge the shy crows pass along.
With bowstring-twang the wild-fowl wing hence their
  arrow-flight,
What time the full-moon lingers above the floor of
  night,
While, last of summer's tokens, new-born to feebler
  glow,
Like love in old age quickened, the dandelions blow.

Oh ! lovely is the springtime, with fragrance of new
  life,
And lovely is the summer, with song and hue at strife,
But blessings smile at parting, the year is then most
  fair,
When its low summons calls it, far whispering down
  the air.
'Tis then on all Ebeeme comes down a wondrous
  light,
Faint golden mists by daytime, the golden moon by
  night ;
Then all Ebeeme's waters, on every wooded strand,
Are drenched with light no sunset stole yet from
  Elfin-Land.
For now is Heaven nearer ; through all the woodland
  round,
No bush but hath its angel, and burneth without
  sound ;
No sound there is, yet voices are haunting all the air,
And some have said, who listened, that God spake
  with them there.

And ah! of one I mind me, to whom indeed there
 spake
An aëry voice that called him from mountain and
 from lake.
Since then two years have vanished, and still the
 seasons keep
Their round of life and slumber, and birth and life
 and sleep.
But vainly drear November may dye the mountains
 blue,
And stain the waves with color no June skies ever
 knew,
Something there was that is not, on mountain, wave
 and shore,
Since one, who knew and loved them, is met by them
 no more.

PRINCE HENRY TO ELSIE.

(Golden Legend, 2; 912-917.)

Me life holds in such grip
That death is doubly death. I should go forth,
As the doomed culprit, yellow from his dungeon,
Is dragged forth blinded to the glare of noon,
Clutching and cursing. But to thee this life
Is but a filmy cloud that veils the sun,
From one that wanders over singing fields,
And death the wind that lifts it.

EBEEME BOATING SONG.

Air—*Trancadillo.*

There are full many lakes,
    Many ponds, too, there be,
But no one that takes
    Such a hold upon me,
As the sweet lake, the fair lake, the pleasant Ebeeme,
With the light on the lilies, delicious and dreamy.

    Here the wind in the pine,
        And the wave on the strand,
    As they meet and combine,
        Make a melody grand, O'er, etc.

    Oh! sweet is the sound
        From the high mountain side,
    Whence our voices resound,
        By the cliffs multiplied, O'er, etc.

    'Neath the light of the moon
        The canoe glides along,
    While the call of the loon
        Wakes anew at our song, On, etc.

    Then Ebeeme, all hail!
        In thy holiday dress;
    May thy founts never fail,
        Nor thy beauty be less. Oh! etc.

Camp Crosby, West Pond, August, 1879.

THE POET'S TREASURE.

THE sky is a mine of gold to-night,
   And none of its wealth is hid, I ween;
For, stuffed with curdled nuggets bright,
   Is the whole broad stretch of the heaven seen.

And men look heedless up, and say,
   "The clouds are yellow and fair to see."
But the poet hears them not, for away,
   Amid that shining drift is he.

His hand bears neither mattock nor spade,
   Nor a bag to put his gettings in.
From the spangled sky the bright clouds fade,
   And the meadow mists rise gray and thin.

But the poet hath gotten him from the sky
   Treasures that neither fade nor pall,
Which the gold of the rich man cannot buy;
   For Heaven gives freely or not at all.

UNTHRIFT.

I've a way,
To my sorrow,
To borrow
From to-morrow,
To pay
To-day.

TO THE MAY-FLOWER.

O DAINTY May-flower, sheen,
   Dear pledge of summer's green,
How lovely art thou still,
   Torn from thy sun-bathed hill
     Serene!

Thou hast a loveliness,
   That ill can make no less,
And good can but enhance;
   Not born of circumstance,
     Or dress.

And sweet is thy perfume,
   Stealing throughout my room,
As when beneath the sky,
   It made the bluff bee spy
     Thy bloom.

Alas! for flower or face,
   That lacks the crowning grace,
The soul-seal of perfume;
   For nothing can assume
     Its place!

Sweet flower, thy pink and white
   Will soon be faded quite;
But not with shape and hue
   Thy beauty dieth too,
     In blight.

Thy breath and bloom shall be
   Part of my life to me,
And all the flowering year
   Henceforth is made more dear,
     For thee.

Thy beauty hath been wrought
   Through being into thought:
So, through all earthly death,
   Is beauty's vital breath
     Safe brought.

LAND-LONGING.

OH! when I was a little boy I loved the country so:
But now I've grown a big boy I may not thither go,
But I must bide within the town, and toil and moil and strive,
For just enough of misery to keep myself alive.
But when I get an old boy, maybe they'll send me back,
Away from tears and toil and sin, from hearts and heavens black,
And lay me down among the flowers, where long ago I lay,
Beside the shining waters,—as free from toil as they.

IN BOSTON COMMON.

Out of the howling wilderness
    Of the crowded city street,
Where hearts wax hard in the shock and stress
    Of weary, struggling feet.

I wander, sick with a hundred cares,
    Into this field of green,
Till over its acres the Healer fares,
    And blesses me, unseen.

The rest-day's holy stillness dwells
    Herein throughout the week;
Though loud the stricken pavement yells,
    And startled engines shriek.

Yet, at the most, a drowsy drone
    Is all that enters here,
A low, monotonous undertone,
    Which heals the wounded ear.

Rest, rest, long rest and sweet release!
    These murmuring lanes of green
Tell of the hundred years of peace,
    Not merely the fifteen.

Nov., 1880.

AN ARROW SHOT.

The stiff string spun, the lithe wood leaped from the silk and laughed.
It struck, and a yelp therewith was wrung from the whining shaft.

THE CROWS.

WEST ROXBURY, MASS.

Out of the north from the Brookline woods,
 The Crows come flying at set of sun,
Benighting the red of aërial roods,
 In tens, in hundreds, or one by one.

The windless chill of a winter eve
 Is crisping the dampness on walk and way,
But high in the lift those black wings give
 A ruddy glitter of lingering day.

How smooth the feathers are lapped and laid,
 In the strong, broad curve of those steadfast wings!
Ha! there is a gap some shot has made,—
 The Crow's reward for the good he brings.

And still as the ranks above me thin,
 Slow dropping over the southern trees,
Out of the north new flocks begin,
 To rise and redden and sink like these.

In kitchen windows the lamplights flare,
 The milkman hurries his nightly round:
What care these bold buccaneers of the air
 For a sluggish life on the stupid ground?

Now all have passed, and the stars to-night,
 Though little the Crows heed gloom or glare,
Will see them huddled by cape or bight,
 Where the tide has left the long flats bare.

There ocean grants them a feeding ground,
    And twice a day a feast they make
On the clams and mussels that there abound,
    And haply a stranded flounder they take.

So fares the Crow in the winter-tide,
    While field and pasture lie stiff and sere;
When spring comes back, and the brown hillside
    Is green with corn, you shall see him here.

Crows are no robbers, they spoil to save,
    Yet curse for blessing they find at the farms,
And lucky for them if the worst they brave
    Is the scarecrow's broomstick at shoulder-arms.

The worm that gnaws at the sprouting seed,
    The locust ravening field and wood,
'Tis of these alone that the Crow takes heed,
    For the farmer's foe is the black Crow's food.

So the Crow bides inland while summer stays,
    And waxes fat, that is, for him;
Yet little he cares when the autumn days
    Dole slimmer rations and still more slim.

He knows that the sea falls twice a day,
    In cloud and sunshine, in frost and rain,
And so, with a laugh, he is up and away,
    Through the winter dusk to the shore again.

CHARLES MILLER COBURN.

ONLY a few short months are fled,
Since to my absent friend I said:

"Friend that sailest now the sea,
Best of wishes follow thee,
And shall follow, even when
Thou hast brought them back again."

Now upon a deeper sea,
Thou art embarked how suddenly!
A sea that hath no landward breeze,
And no returning messages,
Nor any glimpse of other shore,
To us, who strain its blackness o'er.

O friend, how oft in days to be,
Shall men look back and sigh for thee,
Missing, in hours of utmost need,
Thy words to teach, thy steps to lead!

But where thou art there must be good,
Though here not seen nor understood;
And when we too are set adrift,
Toward those low clouds that never lift,
And faith is well nigh lost in fear,
Then will we cry with better cheer;
"Beyond the cloud, come sea, come shore,
We sail to meet our friend once more!"

ANNIVERSARY HYMN.

FOR THE BAPTIST CHURCH IN FREEPORT, MAINE.

Full well and long the Father's hand
    Hath led His people on,
Through storm and sun, o'er desert sand,
    And into Canaan won.

But looking back from year to year,
    For threescore and fourteen,
We see Thee in the desert drear,
    As in the fields of green;

And bless Thee, seeing where of old
    Our wayward steps have striven,
Not less for what Thou didst withhold,
    Than what Thy grace hath given.

A little band, before Thy throne
    Our fathers knelt to pray;
Make us, tenfold in numbers grown,
    Tenfold more strong than they.

Here, from this height of years, we see
    An untried way before;
O Father, hold us near to Thee,
    As in the days of yore:

And ever, if from Thee, O God,
    Our sinful footsteps stray,
In love spare not from us the rod,
    Who turn from love away.

Yet, rather, standing in this place,
  Where Thou so oft hast heard
True prayer of old, we pray for grace
  To heed Thy mildest word;

And may we follow ever thus
  Through all the future's hours;
As with our fathers, so with us,
  Our father's God and ours.

28th Sept., 1881.

EMERSON.

A STAR fell, methought.
  I must have seen it rise;
For lo! next night,
A new star's light
  Lit all the upper skies.

LONGFELLOW.

WHILE all the birds are fluttering in the sun,
  Fluting their sorrow for the singer dead,
What wilt thou do, thou dull and songless one,
  Who yet loved much as they that lowly head?
    "Love and be silent."

REFORM.

HALT! hear ye not the cry,
That voice not loud nor high,
But a mighty undertone,
From the four winds of heaven blown?
Hark! ye can hear it now,
The sound men heard of yore,
Making the tyrant bow,
And crumbling sceptre and throne.
Hark to the gathering roar,
And flee from the coming storm.
Reform, reform, reform!

What! an ye will not hear,
Look the horizon round,
See how the wroth clouds rear
Their blackness from the ground.
The blue sky shrivels in dread,
It is furled as a sail is furled;
There are fiery bolts to be sped,
For the vengeance waxeth warm,
For justice wakes on the world,
And woe to the guilty head.
Reform, reform, reform!

Nay, it is now too late!
Ye heed, but we cannot wait;
The tempest has drawn too nigh;
Its threaded lightnings ply,
And a fiery shroud they weave.
Fools, ye would not believe,
Ye doubted, and ye must die.

Ye vanish, and where ye stood
The hosts of the upright swarm,
Their battle-cry made good:
Reform, reform, reform!

15th Oct., 1882.

LOST.

THERE are three things that most I hate;
The breath of orchards blossom-laden,
The calm eyes of an innocent maiden,
And snow; I think they mock my fate.
The reason you must guess with ease,
But first that apple-blossom, please;
There! in the city's trodden slough,
Will any one call it fragrant now?
Into the street I too was flung,
A blossom;—oh! I still am young,
That is, if you reckon life by years,
And not by harvests of blood and tears.
Don't start; I know my face is a fright,
Though I haven't seen it since one night,
Long gone, when my mirror told such a tale,
That I struck the glass: would life were as frail!
The snow, with its beauty white and cold,
I hate as much as I loved it of old.
It trips so daintily down from the sky,
As if it were proud of its purity.
It blackens soon; for that I am glad,

But soiled or stainless I hate it as bad.
Do you wonder that I cannot brook
The peaceful depths of a maiden's look,
Beholding sin and misery
As with babies' eyes that do not see?
Babies!—ha, ha! no mother am I:
Some secrets keep; you'd best say good bye.

CHRISTOPHER.

Rufus, Rufus, some one calleth thee :—
The night is dark, the river roareth black,
And in the storm the great trees rive and crack ;—
　"Rufus, come carry me!"

Rufus, there calleth thee some little child ;
But merrily the red logs blaze within,
Rest cometh sweet ; it surely were a sin
　To brave a night so wild.

But still he hears the knocking and the cry :
A giant such as thou has naught to fear.
"Come, child, sit squarely on my shoulders here,
　Fear nothing, it is I."

So spake he as the foaming brink he sought,
Scarce knowing if indeed he bore a load ;
Then knee-deep down into the flood he strode,
　Which smote, but stirred him not.

Soon strangely heavy gan to grow his load,
The little child weighed on his neck like lead;
The stream rose higher o'er its slippery bed,
    Yet onward still he strode.

But when the middle of the stream was won,
His little burden weighed like mountains piled,
His shoulders bent beneath the clinging child,
    He scarce could stagger on.

Then, slipping, straightway he began to sink.
"Help me!" he cried; the child stretched out a hand,
And in a moment they were safe at land
    Upon the farther brink.

"Who art thou?" gasped the giant, sore surprised.
"I am the Christ-Child, and thou art no more
Rufus, but shalt be Christopher, who bore
    The sad benighted Christ."

Christ-bearer! oh, how often have we tried
Some little load of duty thus to bear,
Which grew and weighed us down, till, in despair,
    Like thee for help we cried!

How light the burden that we raised so free!
How weak the knees that bowed themselves in pain!
Full many a smallest duty doth contain
    Christ and Gethsemane.

O Christ! once weary, but forevermore
Strong in the splendor of thy saving might,
Be with us through the waters, when, by night,
    We stumble far from shore!

GARFIELD.

O NATION, sitting in the dust
    By him you honored so,
Full well your sorrow; it is just
    Such tribute to bestow.

Full well your flags that kissed the sun
    Droop half-mast dashed with gloom,
And dirges knell, and anthems swell,
    And brazen requiems boom.

Ay, well that mart and hall and dome
    Are hung with mourning's hue,
But better still that shops and home
    Are hushed with sorrow too.

Oh, prayer unanswered, though so fond!
    But see the Father's hand,
Which gives to-day this perfect bond
    Of union through the land.

Oh! not for naught ye wreathe the white
    Above the black of woe;
'Tis standing against Heaven's light,
    That makes Death dark below.

Sept., 1881.

PURITY.

No deed, no word, no thought be mine,
    That I would not to her impart,
Who reigns, sweet human maid divine,
    The empress of my heart.

FALLEN.

"DEAD! my darling, my eldest born,
So strong, so handsome, but yesterday
Kissed me good-bye, and they say this morn
He is dead in the city, and I away.
Why did they tell me so late as this?
A mother's hand should have soothed his brow,
A mother's lips met his farewell kiss,
Her ear caught the words that are silent now.
The best go soonest, ah me, how sure!
My boy, all brimming with love to men,
He would save the race, would have all men pure,
And now they never shall see him again.
But in vain may the sad earth weep and moan,
When Heaven opens to claim its own."

Ah! the saintly mother must not know
How it was that her darling died;
All unworthy a mother's pride.
Dying in horror, stricken low,
With pangs that purity never won,
Died, and was buried with brutal mirth,—
Another plague-spot in the earth,—
And the sunlight was sweeter that he was gone.

CALM.

ALONG the steel-blue knife-edge of the restful ocean's
    rim,
Two ships of cloud and cob-web do unadvancing
    swim.

EVENING.

LIKE an unworded thought the landscape lay,
    Blurred by the fog and shifting formlessly ;
The great elms reached aloft and far away,
    And struck aërial roots into the sky ;
The village vanished with its eastward vane ;
    The pond became an ocean, and the fall
Rumbled unseen ; in wood and flowery plain
    The song-birds and the bees were silent all.

MORNING.

GILDING the mist, the God-smile of the dawn
    Broke over field and flood ; the glistening trees,
Wind-swept, flung down their jewels on the lawn,
    Then raised their hands to greet the blithesome
        breeze ;
The new-mown fields were all pavilioned white
    With shining cob-webs by the mist betrayed.
The golden vapors vanished into light,
    And all the birds a glad-mouthed music made.

MORN.

A THRILL of gladness touched the heart of Day,
And it awoke from sleep, and, kissing, parted
The long and golden lashes of the Morn.

TRUTH.

Truth, I will clasp thee to my breast,
    Though thy pure touch consume in me
The half my heart; I know the rest
    Will beat more gladly, beating free.

Behold, I lay my hand in thine,
    I lift mine eyes to meet thine own,
Though shriveled by that look divine,
    Though lifted to be overthrown.

Oh! give me strength to follow thee,—
    'Tis thou must give, no might have I,—
And I will follow, though it be
    Through martyr-fires of agony.

SIN.

Sometimes, as on a sunny morn,
    Or by the sea, I feel that sin,
Though with my body it were born,
    Yet with my soul has nothing kin.

LOVE.

Ask me not why I love: it is enough
That I may love; so be there no rebuff,
Love seeks requital none, but is content
In pouring itself out, and grows by being spent.

A TWOFOLD TEACHING.

Yellowly out of the blue of the sky,
From the maple branches slender and high,
Sliding and swirling around and around,
The fall's first ripe leaf drops to the ground.

And so the summer is over and gone.
O thin, smooth leaf that I hold in my hand;
And sunset it was that we took for the dawn.
O thin, smooth leaf, who gave you command
To banish the summer yet in its prime,
The fair, sweet summer out of the land,
And to welcome the winter before its time?

O little leaf, as I hold you here,
Methinks in your slender and white-ribbed form,
There lurketh a chill that I cannot warm,
Though I hold you in both my hands pressed close:
Yea, a chill that so but the stronger grows,
Till the warm blood shrinks away in fear,
From a nameless power that it cannot oppose.

'Tis the cringing of life from the conqueror death,
In bleak foreboding of coming doom.
'Tis the soul's withdrawing with bated breath
From the death-shade's damp and evil gloom;
'Tis the world-old feud surviving still,
That driveth my blood from the leaf so chill.

So I toss the wan leaf away from me,
And I think, "O leaf, how calm thou art!"
And I think again, "Thou hast played thy part,
And therefore hath death no terrors for thee."

So I lift my eyes, and turn them aloft,
And see the bough upon which it grew;
And lo! all roughened with leaf-buds new.
Is the branch where the dead leaf swung so oft.

So I look again to the leaf on the ground,
And my heart within gives a throb more glad ;
And I say, " I believe while I spake so sad,
That the life I mourned I should see no more
Has been lying hidden safe and sound.
There on the bough where it swung of yore.
Sheltered safe from the snow and the rain,
And only waiting for summer again,
To blossom more beautiful than before!"

THE OLD MATHEMATICIAN.

ALL day he muttered over straws and sticks.
But could not tell that three and three make six.
Then two times two went from him; but he still
Mumbled and fumbled; by and by fell ill.
With his last breath he sat upright and said:
" The circle squared, how simple!" and was dead.

STORM.

THE lancing lightning thrusteth, the thunder booms
   amain,
And sweeps above the crushed earth the myriad-
   marching rain.

MAY.

*Diffugere nives, redeunt jam gramina campis
Arboribus que comæ.—Horace.*

March, tearful in her smiles, is past,
   And April, smiling through her tears,
And now, spring's fairest month and last,
   The golden-girdled May appears.

The mornings take a softness on,
   That is not kin to winter's light,
The days are slower to be gone,
   But sunset sooner brings the night.

The scentless purity of snow
   Gives way unto the mild perfume
Of buds that burst and leaves that blow
   And blossoms breaking into bloom.

The brook, late bowed with icy yokes,
   Leaps like the squirrel on its brink,
And in the amber air the oaks
   Become a vaporous maze of pink.

The sky takes on a deeper blue
   To match the sun's intenser glare;
And, winging high its clearness through,
   Return the song-birds to our air.

Upon the sunny slopes appears
   A strange, portentous, warlike birth
Of golden shields and jeweled spears,
   Like that which Cadmus called from earth.

But here no dragon's teeth were sown,
   So here no sons of earth uprise;
The dandelion and grass alone
   Salute the wondering traveler's eyes.

A quivering film of living gold,
   Drifting and circling in the sun,
The butterfly we now behold,
   And, greeting, thank her, every one,

For those delicious memories,
   Born, like the sunshine, in the East,
That she recalls, and in them is
   Herself remembered not the least.

O Psyche, teacher sent from God,
   Thou hoverest near, and straight mine eye
Looks deeper than the springing sod,
   Looks higher than the azure sky.

FLOWERLESS.

Some plants there be that never bloom,
By mid-day glow or mid-night gloom:
In summer's heat or winter's cold, .
Nor bud nor blossom they unfold.
Not only in the fields around,
And in the woods these plants are found,
But such full many firesides know,
Fragrant and fair that flowerless grow:—
Because they wait to bloom, I wis,
Beneath some brighter sky than this.

CHILDREN.

A world without any children,—
 What a worn old world it would be!
A dreary life in a world like that
 Would be worse than death to me.

Then come, pink May-buds of children,
 With opening hearts like the morn;
There's hope for earth, and the dwellers of earth,
 While such as ye are born.

EPIGÆA REPENS* CORONATA.

'Tis years since last I saw thy face,
  Epigæa,
In thy wonted dwelling-place,
Made a heaven by thy grace,
  Bella mea.

Bright the blue sky bends o'erhead,
  Epigæa;
Pines their fragrance round me shed.
But 'twas thine my steps that led,
  Bella mea.

---

* Botanical name of arbutus,
 The bonniest bloom spring sends to us;
 Though, really, that wee, pink, hid-away flower
 Smells sweeter by the name of mayflower.

Love beheld thee on the ground,
                    Epigæa.
Through dull robes thy beauty found,
And thy life with fragrance crowned,
                    Bella mea.

Was it for thy beauty he,
                    Epigæa,
Honored thee so royally?
(Never queen was crowned like thee,
                    Bella mea!)

Nay, thou hadst been crowned with less,
                    Epigæa.
Rather for thy lowliness
Art thou made so blessed to bless,
                    Bella mea.

Here I kneel before thy throne,
                    Epigæa.
Woo thee, Sweetest, for mine own,
Place thee in my heart alone.
                    Bella mea.

LOVE IN THE NORTHLAND.

BREATHE loud, breathe low,
Blithe winds that blow
    Betwixt the sun and sea,
And when ye trip
O'er Anna's lip,
    Steal thence a kiss for me.

O star of night,
Burn warm and bright.
   Melt all the dark to gold ;
Thou canst not burn
Like hearts that yearn
   Each other to enfold.

Thou, star divine,
Canst ne'er outshine
   Her eyes, which light my soul.
O winds of south,
Her fragrant mouth
   Hath sweets ye never stole.

ELDORADO.

I AM poor among my neighbors,
   And the rich look down on me,
Even friends that long have known me
   Pity me my poverty.

But although for me too quickly
   Winter follows after fall,
Though my food is coarse and scanty,
   I am richer than they all.

They, perchance, the wealthiest of them,
   Build them ships or buy them land,
Rear them houses ; I have castles,
   Kingdoms, fleets at my command.

They have households, I have nations;
    They have gold in hoarded piles,
I have diamond mountain ranges,
    Lakes of pearl that stretch for miles.

Ruby rivers, skies of sapphire,
    Jasper meadows, emerald trees,
And uncounted bands of yeomen
    Placed in keeping over these.

But, alas! my brave possessions
    Are a wonderful in Spain,
And of all my ships sent thither
    Not one has come back again.

Have they all been stranded, sunken,
    Lured to death by siren charms?
Have the ghostly, gliding icebergs
    Clutched and crushed them in their arms?

Tempest-tost or fog-bewildered,
    Whatsoever fate was theirs,
Nothing know I, and unknowing,
    Still have hope amid my fears;

Often fancying at morning,
    As I gaze upon the sea,
That the white sails seen afar-off,
    Are my ships come back to me.

Often fancying at evening,
    When the light-strikes broad and low,
That within the eastern shadows,
    I behold my banners blow.

And, though often faint with watching,
　　Sick with fears that will not rest,
Still I launch and send my vessels,
　　On their unreturning quest.

Longing, praying, hoping, trusting
　　Through my bitterness of pain,
That they all, a grand armada,
　　One day will come back from Spain;

And, returning, bear me with them,
　　Whither all my treasures are,
In the land of youth eternal,
　　Underneath the morning star.

June, 1879.

TO THE FIRE-FLY.

Strolling watching of the twilight,
Guiding others by thine eyelight;
Lanterned, lone Diogenes,
Coursing curious through the trees;
Delver in the depths of night,
With thy miner's-lamp alight;
Flitting, phosphorescent creature—
Would I had thee for my teacher!
For thou knowest much, I ween,
That no man hath ever seen,
With whatever rich and rare,
Lieth hidden anywhere.

Having thee to go before,
All the forest I'd explore;
And thy taper should disclose
Every secret that it owes;—
Where the grosbeak builds her nest,
Where the owls in daytime rest,
Where the fairies dance in rings,
Where the adders whet their stings,
In what place the rainbow's coiled
Lest its beauties should be spoiled,
What the aspen is afraid of,
What the autumn's dyes are made of.
These, and many more beside,
Would I learn with thee to guide.
But, alas! it may not be.
Only they that cannot see
Have the chance to look, and they
That could see are kept away.
Yet, I fain would thank thee, fly,
For the moments thou art nigh;
Since thou mindest me of what,
All too often, is forgot:
That whoever looks with love
On the meanest of God's works,
Sees a light, which in it lurks,
Imaging the light above.

June, 1878.

THE SINGER.

There came on a time unto me
A song bird from over the sea,
    A friend from a land far away;
Her eyes had the noon overfraught,
While the gold of her tresses had caught
    The last kiss of dawn and the day.

There came unto me on a time
A friend from a far-away clime,
    A song bird from over the sea;
She is gone with the years that are gone,
But the voice of her singing sounds on,
    And never is silent to me.

THE FROLIC OF THE LEAVES.

The leaves of the elm and the maple
    First opened their wondering eyes,
Under the bending beauty
    Of the azure April skies.

They drank in the warmth of spring-time,
    Then threw off their swathing bands
And reached out into the sunlight
    Their pink, imploring hands.

They were rocked in the arms of summer,
    While wandering winds above
Crooned a low lullaby to them,
    In murmuring music of love.

But the drowsy charm of the west-wind
    The leaves threw off ere long,
For they heard in the blue above them
    The bright bird's tempting song ;

And beneath them they saw the greensward,
    With its beckoning blooms, and they sighed
To be out of the lonely tree-top,
    Into the world so wide.

But the mother bade them be patient,
    And wait till the autumn should come,
And then, when their wings were stronger,
    She would let them fly from home.

At last, after watching and waiting,
    Autumn, the beautiful, came,
Stepping with sandals of silver,
    Decked with a mantle of flame.

Then Nature, the loving mother,
    In the moony month of sheaves,
Arrayed in yellow and crimson
    Her children, the forest leaves.

She lingered long o'er their beauty;
    At last, one October morn,
When the ground was sprinkled with frost-pearls,
    And the last of the song-birds had gone.

She spake to them softly and called them,
    While she brushed a tear away,
Which they saw not,—and told them,
    They now might go out and play.

The leaves clapped their hands, delighted,
    And shouted loud in their glee;
Then sprang on the back of the north-wind,
    Which lifted and set them free.

Ha! 'twas a glorious riding,
    As they leaped away with the blast.
Frisking along over fences,
    Scampering gaily and fast;

Racing and dancing and darting,
    Now hurrying back to their home,
Then trooping away to the brooklet,
    Which chased them and splashed them with foam;

Now frolicking high in the sunlight,
    Now whirling low on the ground,
On, without stopping to rest them,
    Onward in merriest round.

So sped they. At last the north-wind
    Began to grow chill and bleak;
Their dresses were torn and faded,
    Their feet were weary and weak.

So Nature, the loving mother,
    Who had watched them with many fears,
Laid them to rest on the brown earth,
    She had softened with her tears;

Then covered them tenderly, softly,
    With snow-blankets warm and deep, —
Her children, tired of playing,
    And weary, and full of sleep. *

Jan., 1878.

OVER-BIRTH.

As the sun in setting rises,
    Sinks into another day,
And our sunset blends with sunrise
    In far-off and fair Cathay;

So we find a birth in dying,
    So we find, when life is done,
And our friends are lost in darkness,
    Passing from us one by one,

And the world grows fainter, dimmer,
    And at last fades all away,—
Not a night in death before us,
    But a bright, eternal day.

THE PATH TO SONGLAND.

Where is the path to Songland?
    For my feet have gone astray,
And day and night I wander,
    And cannot find the way.

O broad, white path to westward,
    Under the sunset's red,
Is thy pavilioned pavement
    Whereon my feet must tread?

So I turn my steps to the westward,
    But, ere ever a mile is done,
The fields of red, o'er the path of white,
    Have vanished with the sun.

O stream that singest forever,
  With tuneful voice and strong,
Thy music, didst thou not learn it
  Within the walls of song?

And, if I follow thee northward,
  Shall I not at last behold
The diamond walls that I see in dreams,
  And the roofs and spires of gold?

But the stream goes on with its music,
  And makes no answer to me,
Till my heart is sick with yearning
  For the land that I may not see.

Then I look far under the morning,
  And gaze on the hills of blue;
And I think, "If I stood on your heights, mayhap
  I could find my way anew."

But scarce have I turned to seek them,
  With heart that would fain be light,
When a mist comes down on the hills of morn,
  And hides them from my sight.

And now return the song-birds
  Back from their southern home,
Leaving a trail of music
  Behind them as they come.

And I think, "Oh! surely, surely,
  The land I seek lies here."
But many a weary mile I've gone,
  And never a step more near;

And so, forever seeking,
    And baffled as ever before,
I said, "The Songland is not for me,
    I will seek its path no more."

And then an angel came and laid
    Upon me a hand of pain,
And straightway were my footsteps bent
    Toward the Land of Song again.

THE WORLD-VOICE.

The great, loud world hath many tongues,
    But voices only one;
It speaketh in the shouting stream,
    And in the silent sun.

One word alone it speaketh aye,
    Below, around, above:—
Hark! even now the maple buds
    Whisper and call it "Love."

SUCCESS.

Put the goal at fifty paces;
    Mark each come in.
Put it fifty score; the race's
    Former laggard's win.

THE POET.

Who is the poet? Who is he
But the man of tears in the midst of glee?
And who is he but the man of mirth
Amid the sorrows and sighs of earth?

He sees too clear, and he sees too deep,
Not to be laughing when others weep;
And he sees too deep and clear by half,
Not to be weeping when others laugh.

RECOMPENSE.

The mills of the gods grind slowly,
   But the mills of the gods grind long.
And under the stars the mill-wheels
   May sing a merrier song.

WANHOPE.

Ashes of roses, ashes,
   And my life is a faded coal,
Where the fires of passion have slackened,
   On the hearthstone of the soul.

Ashes, ashes of roses,
   And my heart is ashes and dust,
While slowly over the love that burned,
   Gathers a whitening crust.

Ashes, my heart is a cinder,
　Blackened, burnt out and a-cold,
That is blown by the gusts of winter
　To its grave in the icy wold.

ANTECEDENTS.

"What was the way?"
Oh! who can say?
A look,
A word,
A book,
A bird,
Sheep's-eyes
And sighs,
A kiss
And bliss,
Then, by and by,
I.

SUNLIGHT.

O Love, in the laugh of the sunlight,
　The doubts of the dark flee away,
The twilight is lost in the one light,
　The dawn-bud in day.

IN TAU KAPPA PHI.

Said Brother A. to Brother B., "Is everything at hand
  To greet our brethren visitant and make their hearts
    expand?
Has Brother D. scoured up the bones and dusted
    out the coffin,
And fixed the skull the same sweet smile it saw the
    fellows off in?
If so, what brings you weeping? Why court that
    solemn vein?
High tragedy is not your hold, I prithee smile
    again."
Then out spake Brown the guileful, oh, Brown that
    man of guile!
"Alas! there's something lacking yet to fit us out
    in style;
We need, as 'twere a sprig of green to deck our
    banquet's crockery,
But everything I've sampled yet has proved a hollow mockery.
Of course I mean a mental green, my words are
    metaphorical,
But all I've tried, as I have said, has turned phantasmagorical."
Here Brother A. shed briny tears to see Brown
    grow pathetic,
And throw his dictionary up without the least
    emetic.
But Brown cried out, "Eureka, I have it, habet
    me!
A poem is the thing we want, I'll get it too, you'll
    see.

I've only just to drop a line to our good Brother K.,
The man that all the Muses love (to have him keep
    away),
And in a trice, as slick as mice, he'll send me back a
    poem,
With every line so full of green 'twill fairly overflow
    'em."
Then Brown the base, bad as his word, sat down and
    wrote the letter.
And this is what K. sent him back,—and wishes it
    were better.

Hail to thee, star-crowned Nourishing Mother,
    Throned amid billows of blossom and foam,
Lo! we come back to thee, brother and brother,
    Children of thine that have wandered from home.

Well has it fared with thee, Ancient in Glory,
    Lightly the years have swept over thy brow,
Sons of thine age grow decrepit and hoary,
    Thou wast ne'er younger nor fairer than now.

Brothers in honor and love reassembled,
    What is the message ye bring from afar?
Weakness that doubted and faltered and trembled?
    Courage that triumphed with many a scar?

Praise not or blame not the day till it's ended;
    Blue skies may smile in the hurricane's track.
Loveliest mornings too often are blended
    With horror of tempest and darkness and rack.

Leave to the rough world its doubt and derision,
    Breathe for one night but the sweet air of love,
Fondly recalling the past's vanished vision,
    Boldly await what the future shall prove.

O ye, the younger, that stand in our places,
    True is the grasp that your greetings bestow,
Loving the welcome that shines in your faces,
    Fondly we hail you with hearts that o'erflow.

All the old joy wakes anew in your presence,
    Hope that leaped forward athirst for the strife,
Faith in mankind, in its princes and peasants,
    Bliss of but breathing, and rapture of life.

Long may the Mother that cherished us meet us,
    High let her sons lift her ancient renown;
Still may we find loving voices to greet us,
    True hands to clasp as in years that are flown.

So, hand in hand, while reluctant we sever,
    This be our pledge in the Tau Kappa Phi:
Truth to our loved Alma Mater, and ever,
    Faith and devotion and love to the Chi.

For the five-yearly reunion of the Chi of the Zeta Psi., Colby University, Commencement, 1885.

TEMPLES.

THE mighty temples built of yore
    Lacked yet the roof on high;
So be thy soul walled round about,
    But open to the sky.

THREE LETTERS.

I.

How I love it! our sturdy old English,
    Which Hengest and Horsa brought o'er;
The speech with the sough of the pine-boughs,
    And the roar on the frore white shore.
I've read to-night tilll I'm nodding,
    And ought to be snugly abed;
But the snow whirls without in the darkness,
    And in-doors the fire-light flames red;
And, somehow, I can't think of sleeping
    Till I've had a talk with my chum.
Do you know it's nigh ten years, old fellow,
    Since we two were graduates glum?
It is, though, and now, next commencement,
    We both must make sure to go back,
To meet round the merry old table,—
    God grant that no face we may lack!
What fun it will be then to meet them,
    And hear what they all have to say!—
The toilers, whose play has been working,
    The drones, who've been working at play.
I can see them now, Fred with his blue eyes,
    And Jack with his dandified air.
(They say Jack is safe for a judgeship,
    And Fred for a congressman's chair.)
But, somehow, our bard has turned doctor,
    Our pitcher has pitched into sin,—
I mean from the pulpit,—they whisper
    That Brooklyn is roping him in.
Then there was our bashful "Sweet William,"
    Shot-proof against feminine tricks,

He's a boarding-school-ma'am's husband somewhere,
    They say that his latest makes six.
And that reminds me how many
    Good fellows are in the same box:
First strung up in Dan Cupid's pillory,
    And then clapped by Hymen in stocks.
Don't you pity them all, the poor fellows,
    To think of the woes they've been through?
Why they are old stagers by this time,
    No longer young bucks like us two.
I'm younger than I was in college,
    And you've not grown older a day.
To be sure, my brush strikes a few gray hairs,
    But for years I've been just a bit gray.
What was it you wrote of a bald spot?
    Oh, nonsense! You must have caught cold.
Take a hot lemonade with a stick in,—
    We bachelors never grow old.
I saw Phil last week in the bosom,
    Etc., etc., one brat.
Tow-headed, with eyes like a pansy,
    Just learning to spell dog and cat.
It's mother I used to meet sometimes,
    Before she became Mrs. Phil.
A plump little yellow-haired creature,
    With a voice like a leaf-dappled rill.
Not so fine, though, as Miss Smith, my neighbor's,
    Her cousin, but younger and much
Better looking, and brainier likewise,
    With gold hair like silk to the touch.
By the way, you should hear her read Cædmon.
    Oh! she can "git inc" with the best.

Fine mind, and no blue-stocking either,
    But socially much in request.
We've just begun reading Beowulf.
    Last evening, to my surprise,—
Would you think it?—The "umbor wesende"
    Brought tears to the dear creature's eyes.
Then Mac, I presume you know, married,
    But she's a brunette, seems to me.
I've no taste for crow-colored tresses;
    But it's lucky we don't all agree.
Well, so the boys launch out and leave us.
    Old fellow, don't you take a flight.
If you do, but of course not, what nonsense!
    Ta, ta! This must do for to-night.

2.

So you ask my congratulations.
    Ah! little had ever I thought,
Since first we clave to each other,
    To be thus by my chum besought.
For I had dreamed of our friendship
    As something that never should wane;
That "passing the love of women"
    Should be the love of us twain.
And I had planned and expected
    That, when the years had gone by,
And we were grown old in harness,
    We should set forth, you and I;
And, boys at heart as aforetime,
    Wander by land and sea.
Together and always together,
    In converse loving and free:

And, at last, when the world was rounded,
    We should drift into some retreat
By the speaking sea and abide there
    Till life its years complete.
Why, so had we spoken together,
    And so I supposed you had meant,
But, presto! a sudden fancy,
    And a life-time's purpose is rent.
I cannot be less than your friend,
    However you deal with me.
I wish you joy; but I cannot
    Forget what I hoped should be.
Nor can I refrain from wishing
    That sometimes, 'mid all your cheer,
You may think of my dreary chamber,
    Which you have made doubly drear.
But I pray to God that never
    By you may be seen or known
The spectre that sits by my hearth-stone,
    In place of the hopes that are flown.

3.

I read the account of the wedding.
    It must have been quite an affair.
But, bless me, how could you stand it,
    With all of that fuss and flare?
Now, we intend to be married
    In the quietest possible way,—
I mean, that is, don't you think so?
    Or, rather, that is to say,—
Confound the heat of this weather!
    If I seem mixed up, that's to blame.

Forgive the way that I answered,
    When first your announcement came.
Just then I was feeling down-hearted,
    And things looked frightfully blue;
But, since then, the sky has brightened,
    And brightened to stay so, too.
I send this to you at Mt. Desert.
    How long are you going to stay?
It might come so we could meet there;
    We leave here a week from to-day.
By the way, do you talk of building?
    I think it's pleasant, don't you?
When the wife keeps the home of her girlhood.
    And needn't begin all new.
But, dear me! I've no time to scribble.
    So, here's to your kin's and kith's
Best health.   I shall have to be going;
    I take tea now with the Smiths.

LOVE'S ARROW.

Oh, say! what wonder of wings is this,
    That flieth hitherward so straight?
Of rainbow and gold, a ferly iwis;
    Alack! the knowledge came too late.

For the shaft of Love, that feathered flew,
    Hath smitten and girt me to the heart;
I thought it a bird of rainbow hue;—
    Oh, strangely sweet is the pang and smart!

AT MY NORTHERN WINDOW.

The sun in winter never deigns
To light my northern window panes,
But, here the revelling storm-winds throw
Their carnival salutes of snow;
And hither, from his polar home,
Comes, brush in hand, the painter gnome,
His icy palette frost-inlaid,
And, deftly blending light and shade,
He brings upon the frescoed pane
The summer's foliage back again.
The pines are white, the willows gray,
The shrubs fantastically gay;
The snow lies crusted on the fields,
The stream its unsung harvest yields,
The shivering day is early gone,
The Bear keeps watch until the dawn.

But, when the new year's bridal white
Is doffed for spring-time's household hue,
My window grants a milder view,
An outlook less unkindly bright.
Oh! sweet in winsome April days
Across the valley-land to gaze,
And strive to mark the viewless line
Where meadow-brown and blue combine.
To right the steady waters roll,
Like the unwinding of a scroll
With runic letters writ upon,—
The logs the current hurries on.

In summer-time the listless trees
Make amorous dalliance with the breeze.
The scaling swallows mount so high,
They seem imprinted on the sky,
The grasses wave, the daisies nod,
The flowers throw kisses at the sod.
Such sights my window shows by day,
But, when the night has frayed away
The day-time gloss, it only brings
A softer loveliness to things.
The stars look out in grave surprise,
Like cradled children's wakeful eyes;
Light-lured, unto my window's height
The beetle spins its winding flight:
Along the river flowing black,
The fire-fly's beacon flashes back;
And lo! far off upon its course,
The night-train, burrowing through the dark,
And flinging back in flame and spark
The blackness into which it bores!

Shy, russet Autumn, Indian maid,
With rubies on thy forehead laid,
Who dost the fickle brooklet teach
Thy low melodious foreign speech,
And, huntress, chasest bow in hand
The song-birds to the southern land;
I see thy footprints, hear the rush
Thy trailing garments make, the hush
That follows when thou passest by,
But thou art viewless to mine eye.
My window shows where thou hast been,

But thou thyself art never seen.
O Northern Landscape, studied long,
In storm and sun, in light and shade;
Take this poor gift of grateful song,
And make the giver overpaid!

Colby University, June, 1878.

FORE-SONG TO BEOWULF.

From the Anglo-Saxon.

WHAT! we have learned of the Gar-Dane kings
    in the days of yore;
Their deeds and the glory thereby, which the noble
    athelings bore.
Often, of scather kindreds, did Scyld the Sceling hurl
Many a band from their mead-seats; great was their
    fear of the earl.
So, after first men found him, an outcast, wrought he
    and strove,
Thence looked for ease unto hardship, and waxed
    under welkin and throve,
Till all men dwelling about him must over the whale-
    road bring
Fees of gold and obeisance: that was a goodly king.
Thereafter, young in his courts, a man-child to him
    was born;
God sent him to gladden the people: He wist of the
    need forlorn,

Aforetime which they had suffered, when a long while
    lordless they dwelt,
Therefore the Glory-wielder world-honor unto him
    dealt.
Beowulf throve and was great, and the Scede-king-
    doms were filled
With the far-heard tale of the welfare befallen the
    heir of Scyld.
So shall a young man work with fees in his father's
    hall,
That, after, when eld is upon him, liegemen may
    dwell at his call,
To fight for his folk in the battle, when come the evil
    days,
For man in every kindred shall thrive by deeds of
    praise.
Then went Scyld the toiler, when the shapen time
    had come,
To enter into the promise and peace of his Master's
    home;
And then it was that his liegemen bare to the water's
    brim
The Scyldings' friend, as aforetime they had been
    bidden of him,
While yet their lief lord's word-sway was mighty in
    the land.
There at hythe stood ready a ring-stemmed ship on
    the strand,
Ice-bright, meet for an atheling, into whose bosom at
    last,
They laid him, the ring-bestower, the mighty, down
    by the mast.

Therein they brought great treasure of jewels from far
    away,
Never of keel yet heard I more comely in array,
With weapons and weeds of battle, with bills and
    with byrnes good.
Gems lay thick on his bosom, the waiting prey of the
    flood.
Not less with treasure they decked him, a nation's
    gifts, than did those
That sent him at first o'er the waters, a child that
    wist not its woes.
Moreover they brought in their homage an ensign,
    wroughten of gold ;
High over head they set it, then drew they forth from
    the hold.
And gave the ship to the billows to bear him far from
    the shore.
Sad were the hearts within them, mournful the mood
    they bore.
And say for sooth can no men, though hall-defenders
    and great,
Heroes under the heaven, who drew to land that
    freight.

SWEDENBORG.

He trod with shodden feet God's altar floor,
    With unanointed eyes
Looked on the Holiest, and forevermore
    Discerned not truth from lies.

THE LORELEY.

From the German of Heine.

I know not what it betokens
    That I am so sad to-day;
There's a legend out of the old time
    That haunts me and will not away.

The air is cool and darkling,
    The Rhine flows calm below,
And the hill-top riseth sparkling
    Into the sunset glow.

A maiden sitteth wondrous,
    Aloft in beauty there:
Her golden jewels glitter,
    She combs her golden hair.

She combs it with golden comb,
    And a lay therewith sings she,
That hath a wondersome,
    Entrancing melody.

In his little boat the sailor,
    With yearning wild, draws nigh:
He sees not the reefs before him,
    He sees but her on high.

I wis the waves will swallow
    The sailor and boat anon;
And that is what with her singing
    The Loreley hath done.

DAVID'S LAMENT OVER SAUL AND JONATHAN.

Slain is the glory of Israel,
Stricken upon thine high places;
How are the mighty fallen!
 Tell ye it not in Gath,
Nor in Ashkelon streets proclaim it;
Lest the foeman's daughters rejoice,
The Philistine maidens triumph.
 Ye mountains of Gilboa,
Let there be no rain upon you,
Neither dew nor fields of offerings;
For there the shield of the mighty,
The shield of Saul was abandoned,
As of the unanointed.
 From the blood of the slain the bow
Of Jonathan turned not back;
From the flesh of the mighty returned not
Fruitless the sword of Saul.
 Lovely were Saul and Jonathan,
Lovely and sweet in their lives;
And in death were they not divided.
Swifter they were than eagles,
And stronger than lions were they.
 Weep, ye daughters of Israel,
Weep over Saul the splendid,
Who clad you in joy of scarlet,
Who decked with gold your apparel.
 How are the mighty fallen,
Slain in the midst of the battle!
Stricken wast thou, O Jonathan,

Fighting upon thine high places.
I am distressed for thee, Jonathan;
Sweet to me wast thou, my brother;
Thy love unto me was wonderful,
Passing the love of women.
  How are the mighty fallen,
And the weapons of warfare perished!

THE DYING HADRIAN TO HIS SOUL.

ANIMULA, vagula, blandula,
Hospes comesque corporis,
Quæ nunc abibis in loca,
Pallidula, rigida, nudula,
Nec ut soles dabis jocos?

TRANSLATION.

WINSOME, wayward spirit guest,
Playmate, whither now thy quest?
Faded eye and faltering lip,
Why no more your laugh and quip?

THE SHEPHERDESS MOON.

From the German of Hoffmann von Fallersleben.

WHO hath the fairest lambkins?
  The golden Moon, I ween,
Who, down behind our tree-tops,
  In heaven dwells unseen.

She comes at latest even,
  When all in slumber lie,
Hither from her fair dwelling,
  Into the peaceful sky.

Then pastures she her lambkins
  Upon its dark, blue meads,
For all the stars so golden
  Are but the flock she feeds.

They never scold nor quarrel,
  But one another love;
Brothers and sisters dwell they,
  The stars in heaven above.

TRANSLATIONS FROM HOMER.

Iliad, 1; 1-5.

The wrath sing, O Goddess, of Achilles, Peleusson,
Deadly, which for Achæans myriad evils won,
And many souls undaunted to Hades sent along;
But gave the heroes' bodies a prey to all the throng
Of dogs and fowls—for suchwise was wrought the will
    of Jove—
From when, at the beginning, fell out the twain that
    strove,
Atreides, king of men, and Achilles the renowned.

Iliad, 8; 555-565.

As when the stars in heaven, about the moon at full
Shine forth in their effulgence, and all the breezes lull;

And crag and peak and hollow stand out before the
  eye,
And all the endless heaven is cloven from on high,
And every star appears, and the herdman's heart is
  light;
So blazed along the Xanthus the Trojan fires at night,
Between the ships and river, with Ilium in sight.
A thousand fires were kindled upon the plain below,
By every fire sat fifty within the ruddy glow.
Beside their cars the horses stood and champed their
  corn
And snow-white barley, waiting the golden throned
  Morn.

The visit of Hermes to the grot of Calypso. Odyssey, 5; 55-74.

But when he neared the island, which far in ocean lay,
There, from the dark-blue deep, landward he bent his
  way;
Until he reached a cavern, within whose lofty dome
A fair-haired nymph was dwelling, whom there he
  found at home.
A fire burned on the hearth-stone, and far the fragrant
  scent
Of cedar cleft, and sandal, along the island went ;
As bright they blazed; within-doors, and singing clear
  and sweet,
She wove her web unwearied, with golden shuttle fleet.
Around the rocky cavern a clustering forest stood,
Of alder trees and poplars, with fragrant cypress
  wood;
Within whose branches nested the wild-birds broad
  of wing,

Owls and hawks, and sea-crows forever chattering,
That ply upon the waters their daily tasks. Here too
Above the hollow cavern a thrifty vine upgrew,
Luxuriant with clusters beneath its cooling green.
Four springs that flowed together, with water swift
    and sheen,
Hither and thither wandered with many a gleam and
    and gloom.
On either hand broad meadows basked in the fragrant
    bloom
Of violet and parsley. Well an immortal had
Beheld the scene with wonder and in his heart been
    glad.

IMITATIVE LINES.

Iliad, 1; 33-34.

So he spake, and the elder, fearing, said no more,
But went his way in sorrow by the loud resounding
    shore.

Iliad, 1; 49-50.

Dire a clang gave the silver, arrowy noy o' the joy
O' first the mules for burden, and hounds for the
    hunts' employ.

TRANSLATIONS FROM VERGIL.

Æneid, 1; 1-7.

OF arms and the man I sing, from Trojan coasts that, of yore,
To Italy, fate-driven, and the Lavinian shore,
Came, after many tossings o'er lands and on the deep,
By power of the gods, for Juno's wrath that would not sleep;
And war-toils bore he many to found him there a home,
And bring his gods to Latium: the Latin folk thence come,
And thence the Alban fathers. and walls of lofty Rome.

Æneid, 4; 700-705.

Therefore dewy Iris, on saffron wings through the skies,
Trailing athwart the sunlight a thousand various dyes,
Downward flew, and. standing above her head, quoth she:
"This lock to Dis I carry, and thee from earth set free."
So spake, and with her right hand she cut the tress; anon
Both warmth and life departed and to the winds were gone.

GERMAN LOVE SONG OF THE TWELFTH CENTURY.

Du bist mîn, ich bin dîn :
Des solt du gewiss sîn.
   Du bist beslozzen
   In minem herzen :
Verlorn ist daz slüzzelin :
Du muost immer drinne sîn.

Thou art mine, I am thine ;
Thereof shalt thou doubt resign.
   Locked thou art
   In my heart,
Lost is the keyikin ;
There must thou ever bin.

THE LANDLADY'S DAUGHTER.

From the German of Uhland.

THERE came three comrades over the Rhine ;
At a goodly tavern they turned them in.

"O mistress, hast thou good beer and wine,
And where is that fair young daughter of thine?"

"My beer and wine are fresh and clear,
My daughter lies on her burial bier."

And when they entered the silent room,
In a coffin of black she lay in the gloom.

The first, he drew the veil away,
And mournfully gazed on the lifeless clay.

"Oh! wert thou yet living upon the earth,
Sweet maid, I would love thee from this time forth.

The second covered the face that slept,
And turned away from the sight, and wept.

"Alas! thou art lying upon thy bier,
And I have loved thee so many a year!"

The third one lifted the veil anon,
And kissed her upon her mouth so wan.

"I loved thee ever, I love thee today,
And I will love thee for ever and aye!"

PERSISTENCE.

From the Swedish of Runeberg.

At a maiden's window stood a young man,
Three livelong evenings in succession,
Knocking and beseeching for admittance.
On the first night he got threats and scolding,
On the second, parley and entreaties,
On the third he got the window opened.

21st July, 1887.

THE GAUNTLET.

(A gorge in northern Maine.)

A BATTLE-GROUND where gods and fiends made war,
    In the old days of mystery and night,
    Gouged out with trampling of the furious fight,
    And strown with hill-tops hurled down from afar,
The battle's hasty weapons; a deep scar
    Upon the brow of this fair land bedight
    With summer's beauty; oh! it is a sight,
    First among those that unforgotten are.
But earth is kind, for now, with foaming brink,
    A swift stream sweeps the glen, striving for aye
    To wash the war-stains off; each rift and chink
Blue, matted berries cover from the day;—
    Only, by night, the weeting, white stars shrink,
    Above the pines, measurelessly away.

THE LION OF LUCERNE.

(Memorial tablet at Colby University.)

MOTIONLESS sufferer, rigid with the thrill
    Of thine immortal anguish! Looking on thee,
    Thy dauntless eye's slow glazing I can see,
    And hear therewith the thickening life blood spill
Out of that mighty heart fast waxing still;
    While on thy brow is knit indelibly
    The overmastering might of agony
    In wrestle with the everlasting will.

O mother land! The swift years come and go,
   But nevermore the glad sun's light again
   Shall look on these whose names are writ below;
And yet, as sweet to them were sun and rain,
   The west wind blithe, as unto us, whose gain
   And glory is, that they have suffered so.

JOAQUIN MILLER'S SONGS OF THE SIERRAS.

HOT-BLOODED bard, whose dizzy, leaping thought
   Sometimes will blind the eye that guides the hand;
   Poet of passion, thou, at whose command,
The hands clench and the cheeks are fever-fraught,
Or swift tears rush into the eyes unsought;
   I hear thy singing from a foreign strand,
   And, listening, feel my landscape's walls expand,
And thank thee for the visions thou hast brought.
For, as I read thy book, before me blow
   Black western pines bent by the mountain breeze;
   Smoke-shrouded prairies, hot and wrathful, flow
In crackling floods, beneath white hills that freeze;
   Gray canyons gloom, and, on a sudden, lo!
   The twittering sheen of twinkling tropic seas.

ILIONEUS.

(A cast in the Boston Art Museum.)

Poor plaster manikin, with scarce enough
  Of shape to show they meant thee for a man,
  Head, arms, feet gone! but yet, methinks I can,
  With thee before me, see the onset rough
Of god and goddess wroth, the stern rebuff
  Of hands that prayed and afterwards began
  As they would fend those arrows, which outran
Thy fear-stayed flight with fell and sleety sough.
Alas for thee! even for thy beauty's sake,
  Which in thy mother waked that fatal pride
That doomed thee and thy brethren swift to fall.
O hapless, having beauty, not to take
  Strength corresponding! Thou proclaimest wide:
  "Rival the gods in nothing or in all."

PHOSPHOR.

To F. S. H.

O lover of the beautiful and true,
  O son of Hellas and the Orient, thou,
  With eyes of star-lit midnight, and with brow
  Of morning; thou art taken from my view,
And half my life has vanished with thee too.
  The voices of the wood and river now
  Sound strange unto me, and, I know not how,
  All things deserted seem, the landscape through.

I watch the Morning brush her darkling hair
    From her bright face, and then I think of thee,
    Who art beneath the sunrise, and, in prayer,
I look to Him that wept at Bethany
    From human friendship, seeking that His care
    Around thee and thine own may constant be.

HESPER.
To Emily.

LIKE a spent bullet to the target's rim,
    The sun drops down into the west; and soon,
    With brandished scimitar, the crescent moon
Wrests the horizon's treasured gold from him.
A lighted taper on the pine's dark limb,
    The star of evening hangs; with velvet shoon,
    And trailing robe of sable, star bestrewn,
The night glides onward, fragrant, vaporous, dim.
Sweet Hesper, far-off friend, around whose head
    The happy beams of sunlight linger yet,
    My thoughts, flown westward with the day that fled,
Would fain seek heaven and the promise get,
    . That thus shall life its light around thee shed,
    When long for me its latest ray has set.

PRICELESS.

LOVE cannot be bought,
    Neither hath it price;
It seeks not, and is given unsought,
    A glad self-sacrifice.

MY WORSHIP.

A TEMPLE that was not made with hands,
Roofed by the sky, and floored by the sands;
Upon whose wave-worn altar-stone,
An awful white, the great sun shone;
Wherein all day the boughs that swang,
Of the mild-heart Christ an anthem sang,
And a sermon sounded, grand and sweet,
In the ocean's multitudinous beat,
And the white wings, flashing athwart the air,
Were the rippling robes of the Angel of Prayer,
And the moon that rose from the ocean's breast,
Was the outstretched hand of God that blest;—
Such is the spot from the world away,
Where I have worshipped my God to-day.

SONG-BIRTH.

BEYOND the beach's trodden slope of sand,
    Down past the frothy, shifting water-line,
    Deep underneath some fathoms of the brine,
    A crystal spring rolls up sweet waters, bland,
Fresh amid all the saltness of the strand.
    No ebb-tide ever lets the sunlight shine
    Unblurred upon it, and around it twine
    Dark, slimy weeds by west-wind never fanned.
So in the poet's heart, amid the gross
    And brackish bitterness of earthly tides,

The well-spring pure of song forever flows,
Sweetening all wherethrough it mingling glides;
   For, though its life streams up through sunless
      woes,
Its birth was on the hills where light abides.

MILTON.

It was the fair, white season of first snow,
   When Milton, bard of purity, was born,
   When, like a snow-flake through the sky of morn,
   His soul, descending, caught the sunrise glow,
And, flushed with beauty, reached the earth below.
   There clad in flesh, whose features yet adorn
   The halls of art, it dwelt till, toil-worn,
   It sought again the skies it erst did know.
O Milton, thou hast only half thy praise
   In having lowered the heavens within man's ken:
   Thine other, equal labor was to raise
The human spirit up to heaven again;
   So, underneath thy forehead's aureole blaze,
   Thine awful eyes are mild with love to men.

UNCONSCIOUS BEAUTY.

The rose knows not that it is fair;
   It only knows,
     Where'er it grows,
All creatures are the happiest there.

MY GALAHAD.

"God make thee good as thou art fair;" thuswise
  Was Galahad the beautiful made knight;
  And riding forth, begirt with Christ's own might,
  He smote the proud and made the lowly rise.
Such favor found he in his Master's eyes,
    That ever went before him day and night
    The Holy Vessel, and its heavenward flight
  Was at his own departure to the skies.
God make thee good as thou art fair, my friend,
    As loving as thou love-enkindling art,
    As bold as thou art brave, make thy life's end
To right the wronged and bind the broken heart,
  And once more shall the Holy Grail descend
To dwell with men, till thou like him depart.

THE TOWN CLOCK.

Day after day, above the market-place,
    Thou standest looking on the throng below;
    Night after night, above thee, still and slow,
  The bannered constellations westward pace.
By day, thou dealest with the insect race
    Of men, that come and look on thee and go;
    By night, the dark hours from thy bosom flow
  To mingle with eternity and space.
The spire above thee rears its masonry,

As if its thin shaft were a monument
Over the wasted moments that must lie
Within thy chamber, evermore unspent;
And still thy flaming finger writes on high
The hurried summons of each moment sent.

A SUMMER'S DAY.

Up from the east came the sun, and a wind from the
    west came to meet him;
All day long, over fields of bloom, blew the wind to
    the eastward,
All day long rode the sun through sapphire skies to
    the westward;
Then came the evening calm, and the wind dropped
    into the ocean;
Then came the evening dim, and the sun sank over
    the mountains.

JOHN BROWN.

The sea-bound landsman, looking back to shore,
    Now learns what land is highest;—not the ring
    Of hills that erewhile shut out everything
    Beyond them from him; these are seen no more;
Nor yet the loftier heights that, from the lower,

He saw far inland, blue, and, worshipping,
   Believed they touched the sky; the gull's white wing
   Long since flashed o'er them sunk in the sea-floor.
These were but uplands hiding the true height,
   Which looms above them as they sink, and rears
   Its greatness ever greater on the sight.
So thou, beyond the widening sea of years,
   Aye risest great, while ever low and slight
   They wane that smote and slew thee in their fears.

BY THE SEA.
To F. H. B.

DEAREST, I thought to-day if I might win
   A name, and then should die, and thou abide,
   Rich with that beauty which is glorified
   By something more than beautiful within;
And men should read my book, and see therein
   How dearly thou wast loved of him that died,
   And haply they should speak it, to thy pride,
   How sweet this were! but stranger things have been.
O Love, the sea is creeping up the beach,
   The buttercups and daisies breathe on me
   Their meadow-fragrance, while they mingle each
Its sweetness with the brine-breath of the sea.
   Dear girl, what dream was that I sighed to reach?
   No recompense for love save love can be.

RUS IVIT.

In memory of Eliza P. Austin.

She's gone into the country;—so it is
    We see her not, nor hear her when we call,
    Nor ever on our ears her accents fall,
But heart and home her gracious presence miss.
She's gone into the country; out of this
    Dark city of Earth, where sights and sounds appal,
    Rush, roar and strife and tears, and, over all,
The smoke that shuts out the eternities.
But in that country, ah! that heavenly one,
    What light and fragrance! What melodious breath!
    What clasping of dear hands, reunion sweet
Of loves unfaded! What new joys begun,—
    Haply to stray with sweet Elizabeth,
    Or sit, like Mary, at her Master's feet!

20th Nov., 1886.

UNA SANCTARUM.

In holier ages men had called thee saint;
    Through thee the blind had been restored to sight,
    Thy name pale lips had whispered day and night,
    In lonely cell, chapel or cloister quaint;
Thy meekness Raphael had aspired to paint,
    And Dante had beheld thee in the light
    That nearest shines to the ineffable bright,
    Where purest souls see God without restraint;

And, born untimely to our evil days,
  Still hast thou kept thy sainthood and its powers,
  Thou sowest heart's-ease by life's stony ways,
Thou bringest morn where midnight blackness lowers,
  And on thy heavenly forehead fall the rays
  That wrap thee with another day than ours.

DAYSPRING.

WIDE o'er the country the morning is breaking,
  Over the green world, under the blue;
The skirts of the west-wind the dew-drops are shaking
  From leaf-tip and bough-tip, the wide woodland
      through.

The bright bobolink, in a bower of blossoms,
  Is scattering music as liquid and bright
As the diamond drops, from the fragrant bosoms
  Of spruce and of hemlock, swept into light;

And I know not what of the four be sweetest:
  The odorous orchard's blushing white,
The bubbling trill wherewith thou greetest,
  Blithe bobolink, the awakened light.

The brindle dawn over miles of meadow,
  Far-flashed from the western hill-tops dun,
Or the dazzling dew that leaps from the shadow
  Into the outstretched arms of the sun.

OUTSHONE.

A NAME how fair! Who ever dreamed
   A face could yet be fairer?
A name how ugly! So I deemed,
   When once I saw its wearer.

Her beauty kindles with a glow
   No dawn e'er caught; and yet,
When once her heart and mind you know,
   Her beauty you forget.

POTENCIES.

   THE shepherd's crook,
   The fisher's hook
   Are stronger far
   Than armies are;
   The student's book,
   The dreamer's nook,
   The maiden's look
   Oft make or mar
   Wider than war.

THE CONSTITUTION.

OUR frigate's high renown
   Shall stem the tide of death,
When her stars have drifted back to the sky,
   And her brazen lips are a breath.

O HEART, AND MUST I SING TO THEE?

O HEART, and must I sing to thee,
    And may not tell thee nay?
For still thou askest song of me
    And wilt not go thy way.

What biddest thou? to sing of love,
    Or yet of woe to sing?
To tell how all below, above,
    I greet with welcoming;

And how I love the sea and land,
    The hill-tops and the sky,
The sunset on the foam-frilled strand,
    The trailing stars on high;

The glorious challenge of the storm,
    The driving rain's caress,
The air upholden snow-flake's warm
    Infolding tenderness;

And how I love the darling few,
    My friends, who hold me dear,
The distant whom of old I knew,
    And, later loved, the near?

O heart, so rich in loving so,
    Let this be then thy strain.
Sad heart, thou beatest low,
    And I must sing of pain.

TO PRINCESS EYEBRIGHT IN THE CATSKILLS.

(With a copy of Idun.)

A star-like shadow gems the mountain's brow,
Slow-twirling, swung beneath the marble cloud,
Above the misty ledges. Stair by stair,
The great pines climb into its cooling shade;
The dales draw down the blue dusk far within them,
The sharp crags fold it tightly to their bosoms,
While all the wide, bright valley upward yearns,
Lured to those fair, far, azure heights that beckon.
Below, the thick-leaved poplars droop with dust,
But, on the heights, the star, become a crown,
Lingers a moment on the sharpest peak,
Then sinks beyond, and all the mountain lies
Wrapped in the wavering blue of airy distance.

O darling child, whose angel, woman face
These ten sweet years hath·robbed the mountain's
       beauty,
Until thine eyes are bluer than its dales,
Thy locks have shorn the sunset, and thy voice,
From heights of being that o'ertop the hills,
Comes down to us and fills our lives with music;
Thou bringest love and light and melody
Into my life; I bring thee here a song.

∴ IDUN ∴

—OR—

THE MEETING WAYS.

THE WEBSTER WOVE IN HIS WEAVING THE WEFT OF AN ELFIN
    TIME,
WITH THREADS OF THOUGHT AND PASSION AND THE SHUTTLE-
    WORK OF RHYME.

Characters in the Play.

Magne, a king.
Gunlad, his queen.
Idun (pronounced E′-doon), their daughter.
Hermod, a prince.
Hyndla, a fairy.
Grendel, a witch.
Earls.
Lords, ladies and attendants.

FORE-SCENE.

The witch GRENDEL, *sitting before her cave, writes on a leaf, then tears it in two and throws the halves to the winds.*

GRENDEL.

Off! 'tis Grendel bids you fly,
   Sunder hearts by heaven united;
Haste, hie! for where ye lie,
   Hearts shall break and hopes be blighted.

ACT I.

KING MAGNE *on his throne, his queen beside him; before them a cradle, courtiers standing about.*

KING.

The moon that made our daughter's birth
Behest of harvest unto earth,
Again has thrust into the night
Its shining sickle silver-white;
And now the merry morn again
Has waked the birds of wood and plain,
And with the music and the light,
Blithe heralds of a life as bright,
We wait the blessing on our child
Of her that dwells by stream and wild.

A delicate rainbow-flush fills the room, and the fairy HYNDLA *enters.*

Dread princess,—

HYNDLA.

    Thou hast sought me, king.
What is thy prayer? No idle thing,
I trust, else dread upon thy land
The wrath of my unpitying hand.
Drought shall parch thy fields to rock,
Famine wither drove and flock ;
Want shall rage, till thou requite
Hyndla for thy mortal slight.
Thou tremblest ; name thy prayer.

KING.

      Most dread.
Who rulest cloud and fountain-head.
No idle wish impels my prayer,
Nor rashly nor unmeet I dare
To crave thy grace. What other shrine
Stands heaped within this land as thine ?
Nor ever did my folk refuse
To pay thee thank of yearly dues.
Therefore I beg thou wilt not scorn
To bless my daughter eldest born.

HYNDLA.

Happy the land whose joy shall be
To shield itself by honoring me ;
Happy thou, when breaking day
Hailed thee father with its ray ;
Happier the coming years, which beam
With joys that pale the present's dream ;
And happiest thou, sweet maid, of all,
Thou whom men shall Idun call,

On whose sleeping brow I set,
Like jewels in life's coronet,
Beauty, truth and gentleness,
Love that lightens but to bless,
Loftiest thought and lowliest mood,
Dwelling in sweet sisterhood,
Woman-heart of sacrifice,
Woman-soul to strive and rise,
Woman-strength to lift and stay.
Strongest in the weariest day.
Sunshine of the home art thou,
Such the jewels on thy brow,
But the brightest gem shall be
Thy maiden modesty.

Here a torn leaf flutters through the open window and alights upon the baby's forehead. The fairy, startled, picks it up and reads:

"Only seeking mayest thou wed."

The queen shrieks, the king staggers back.

KING.

Speak what mean these words of dread?

HYNDLA.

Their meaning all too plainly runs;
Woe is me my benisons!
She that I decreed so meek
Must not wed until she seek;
Seek she cannot, for, alack!
Elfin gifts return not back.

KING.

Name to me the evil doer;
Force shall wring redress and cure.

HYNDLA.

Peace! No mortal here hath wrought,
This despite hath Grendel sought,
Foulest witch of those that dwell
By the steaming mouth of hell,
Whose prevailing word, once spoken,
Never may be crossed or broken;
But obedience oft may shun
What with strife must still be done;
And the seasons that await
Much may hold of kindlier fate.
This be then thy hope; thou hast
Hyndla's friendship true and fast,
And with fearless eye behold
Future days and years unfold.

ACT II.

Twenty years later. A wood. In the background a thicket with two paths joining in front of it. HERMOD *and his earls, riding out to hunt, meet* IDUN *surrounded by her maids and attendants. Her party has entered at the right.* HERMOD *and his party come in at the left.*

EARLS.

Ha, ha, ha, well said, my lord!

Hermod catches sight of Idun, *and a look of delighted wonder leaps into his face, as if a new world had flashed upon him. The two parties ride slowly by each other,* Hermod *staring at* Idun, *and she meeting his look with a rapt gaze of glad self-surrender. As soon as the earls notice* Hermod's *look, the eldest tries to withdraw his attention.*

1st Earl.

I' faith, my liege, a lightsome word.
I do recall a merry tale:
A king, whose sight began to fail,
Would have new eyes. He bids men call
His leeches, craftsmen, clerks and all;
Then states his want, a pair of eyes;
The same he bids their skill devise.—

Hermod pays no heed to the earl, except to repel him with gestures, but keeps his eyes still fixed upon Idun, *until she is hidden from him by the trees; when he recovers himself with a start, and at the last word they ride off.*

ACT III.

Night. Courtyard of a castle. Hermod, *in hunting costume, comes forward.*

Hermod.

Still darkness! Will it ne'er be day?
How slowly drags the night away!
Ah! many a morn the hunt's delight
Has drawn me forth ere fled the night,

But now I seek a nobler chase.
How paltry, trivial, mean and base
Now seem the sports that thrilled my blood,
Ere that blest meeting in the wood!
Four days,—four centuries,—have crept,
Since o'er my soul that vision swept,
And childhood with its toys has fled;
Impetuous manhood comes instead.
In all the wide, waste universe,
But two souls wander, mine and hers;
Nor all the rocky steeps that rise,
'Twixt nether ocean and the skies,
Shall sunder from my riven soul
That sweeter self that makes it whole.
Deep will I drink of bliss to-day,
Or travel far that shining way.
 He walks about absorbed in revery.
But why that strange dislike I found
To seek again the enchanted ground?
Scarce with threats have I arrayed
My huntsmen for the forest glade,
Who vied but lately to fulfill
The lightest whisper of my will.
Untaught am I such words to hear.
But, soft! I mark their footsteps near.
I'll list unseen, perchance to learn
What wrought them this rebellious turn.
  HERMOD *goes out. Earls, in hunting costume, enter.*

1st EARL.

Poor lad! it's found him out at last.
No wall so high, no door so fast,

No shield of proof so stout and stark,
But love's light shaft will find its mark.

2d EARL.

Ah! well I mind me of the day
When Hermod in his cradle lay,
And all stood round with hearts aquake,
What time the fay her blessing spake.
Then, at the last, when hearts grew light,
That fatal leaf of curse and blight,
Slow fluttering on the baby's head:
" Unsought mayest thou never wed."
And then the shrieks, the groans, the tears;
While Hyndla, helpless to their prayers,
Might not her word recall again,
That made him manliest of men,
Nor might she bring the curse to naught,
That doomed him not to wed unsought.
But this 'tis willed he shall not know,
Lest knowledge work his overthrow,
Nor must he love, a danger worse,
Lest blind he rush upon the curse.

3d EARL.

Yet now he loves, and ours the toil
That love by kindly craft to spoil.
But lo! the morn's bright spears advance;
To horse, and to our journey's chance!

They go out. HERMOD *rushes forward.*

HERMOD.

Have I been dreaming? Heaven and earth!
Accursed and shadowed from my birth!

Doomed not to love? No! bitterer wreak,
Doomed to love, but not to seek.
Doom! overthrow! all for a word
The meanest hind speaks undeterred;
For nothing, for the commonest thing
From clouted churl to sceptred king.
I alone must hold my breath,
And love, and gnaw my heart to death!
Nay, may accept! as if my heart
Would play the meeching maiden's part:
As if my soul would link its choice
To brazen lips and bellowing voice.
And if I speak, what then the doom?
No worse than dying. Then, death, come!
Better breathe out my soul in bliss
In one first, last, death-welcoming kiss,
Than live a hundred years of sloth,
Matched with a being that I loathe.
My huntsmen call. Come, Furies fell;
Your shafts may slay; they cannot quell.
He goes out.

ACT IV.

A room in KING MAGNE'S *palace.* IDUN, *playing on her lute, sings.*

IDUN.

Droop and darken, eyes of blue,
Love hath only tears for you.
    Love, begone, and lightly flee,
    Since thy smiles are not for me.

Lips of scarlet, quench your fire,
Torches vain of love's desire.
    Love, begone, and lightly flee,
    Since thy sweets are not for me.

Sink, ye swelling breasts of snow,
Baby fingers ne'er to know.
    Love, begone, and lightly flee,
    Since thy fruits are not for me.

She throws aside her lute, weeping. After a time speaks.

IDUN.

I waste the night in tears; the day,
In tears and heartache, wears away.
Alas! how changed from what I knew,
Ere love into my bosom flew,
And all my life's long curse awoke,
And slew my joy with levin stroke,
And life, which scaled the heavenly wall,
But mounted for a deadlier fall.
Out o'er the shining woods I look,
Toward that blest spot, enchanted nook,

Where first my soul knew joy, and oh!
Where first my spirit felt its woe.
Those rocking branches welcome wave;
I go, perchance some pang to save,
While for a moment I regain
The joy that taught me all my pain.

She goes out.

ACT V.

A wood. Scene as before, but nearer. HERMOD *comes in at the left.*

HERMOD.

Here is the spot. The sky is blue;
The warm sun sifts these branches through,
The birds make music; all is here,
But all is desolate and drear.
The sun, the song, the heavenly light
With her that fled have taken flight.
Blest ground whereon her feet have pressed!
'Twere sweet even now to sink to rest,
Where haply o'er my lifeless head
Her wandering steps might sometimes tread.
Not yet! Come, death, but not till I
Have drunk love's immortality.

Some prompting bids me haunt this ground ;
Yet hence, not here, must she be found.
Perchance at hand the pathway lies
That bore her homeward from my eyes.

He goes out. IDUN *enters at the right.*

IDUN.

So many steps, so much of grief!
Remembered joy brings small relief.
Oh! that I, a peasant maid,
Might meet my lover unafraid,
And might be wooed and coyly won.

HERMOD *re-enters at the left.*

HERMOD.

Another look ere I have done.
Oh! death, oh! bliss a churl to be,
Who welcomes love and speaks it free!

HERMOD *and* IDUN *draw nearer without seeing each other. A soft rainbow-flush steals over the back of the scene, and* HYNDLA *enters behind them.*

BOTH.

Oh! happiest the humblest lot,
Where fate and sorrow enter not,
Nor griefs of greatness e'er annoy,
But love walks hand in hand with joy.
Oh! might I meet my love as he (she),
Whose heart leaps out: "I love but thee!"

At the last words they rush forward and meet in each other's arms. After a first rapturous embrace, the lovers separate and stare at each other bewildered. HERMOD *gazes bitterly at* IDUN, *as if he were the victim of a delusion.* IDUN, *distrusting her eyes, steals up to* HERMOD *and tests his reality by a kiss. He doubts no longer, but folds her to his bosom. Then, with their arms about each other, the lovers turn toward the fairy, who gives them her blessing.*

HYNDLA.

Now, at last, the ban is broken,
She that could not speak has spoken,
He that must not woo has sought.
So hath love deliverance wrought.
So have I my word fulfilled,
And the blessings that I willed,
While the joys I gave of yore,
Fourfold on them I restore,
Joys that every pang remove,
And the crown of all is love,

HUMOROUS POEMS.

THE PIRATE HORSE-CAR.

It was the midnight horse-car,
  That out of Boston sped,
To Roxbury town it took its way;
Ah! black with storms had been that day,
  But worse was just ahead.

Ten passengers that horse-car held,
  And two were children small.
Alack the day, and well-a-way,
  That such should them befall!
But truth's my tale, I must not fail
  To tell, to tell it all.

I. Fitt was the conductor's name,
  U. Bett the driver hight;
With such a pair in charge of them,
  Men had no thought of fright;
They had no fear,—but wait and hear
  The tale that I shall write.

Yet listen first and learn from me
  What sort of folk they were,
That braved the terrors of that night,
  Full early to occur:
A carpenter, a merchant man,
  A tailor and his wife,
A clerk, a scholar and a cook,
  A butcher with a knife,
Two children small; and these were all,
  That rode that night for life.
The carpenter held in his hand
  A saw-set and a rule,

The tailor had a pair of shears,
    His wife, a folding stool,
The scholar held a book, the clerk,
    A pile of magazines,
The cook, she bore a mighty bag,
    Whereon was printed, "Beans."

You've guessed it was a Friday night;
    And midnight was the hour,
The stars were hid, the lamps were dim,
    The wind had lost its power.
Blackness was over all the earth,
    And all was still, save—Hark!
What nearing roar is that they hear
    Behind them in the dark?
A clattering and a grinding noise,
    A grating, fearful roar;
At dead of night no soul of them
    Had heard the like before.

And, while they wondered at the sound,
    The back door open flew,
And in the scared conductor rushed,
    With cheeks of ghastly hue.
"It is the awful Pirate Car!"
    With chattering teeth he said,
Then fainted flat upon the mat,
    And lay as he were dead.
    "O driver, driver, speed thee now,"
    The folk all cried aghast,
"The Pirate Car, the Pirate Car
    Is gaining on us fast;
So spare not voice, nor whip, nor rein,

To make the critters go!"
Then all rushed backward to look out
　　And eye the dreaded foe.
A car of black, too well it showed,
　　And drawn by steeds of black.
They heard the sooty driver laugh,
　　They heard his whip-lash crack,
And, looking up, they saw, above,
　　One red lamp burn alone,
While under it, in ghastly white,
　　A skull and cross-bones shone.
All else was dark, but in the car
　　They heard the smothered cry
Of savage lips that thirsted blood,
　　And still the sound drew nigh.
Then turned they all and cried, "O haste!"
　　The driver, undismayed,
Spoke not a word, but up and down
　　He plied the limber braid.
Yet on the Pirate came, and soon
　　The children both had fits,
The tailor then began to weep,
　　The scholar lost his wits,
The merchant took his wallet out,
　　And threw his cash away,
The women screeched, the butcher swore,
　　The clerk began to pray.
The driver hollaed from the front,
　　"Five minutes, and we're safe!"
But nigh the pirate team had come,
　　They heard its gearing chafe.

Then rose the doughty carpenter,
    And clutched a strap o'erhead,
A lusty man was he and strong,
    These were the words he said:
"I see a way to save us all,
    The beans upon that seat,
We throw 'em out upon the track,
    Their horses stop to eat,
But we keep on."—The passengers
    Now all began to cheer,
Then turned toward the cook and cried,
    "The beans, oh! give 'em here."
"Alas, alas!" the cook replied,
    "The beans I may not spare;
They are for breakfast Sunday morn,
    And who of us would dare,
On Sunday morn, to miss that rite,
    Which over all the land,
From Caribou to Danbury,
    Is held the first command?"
Then all, with horror-stricken eyes,
    Forbore to touch the fruit,—
Oh, fruit of transcendental power,
    So cosmic in repute!—
And in the hush they heard outside
    The Pirate's grim salute:
"Ho! car ahoy, down brakes, hard down,
    Heave to, and take in sail!"
And then the pirate team they heard
    Cribbing the hinder rail.
But, while they listened, through the car
    The driver darted past,

And in a trice unto the rail
    The pirate span made fast;
Then, stepping over on their backs,
    Unshipped the whiffle-tree,
Before the pirate driver guessed
    What might his purpose be.
Then he leaped back and grabbed his reins:
    " Hurrah, hurrah, we're saved!"
But fierce and loud the pirate crew
    In baffled fury raved.
For well they knew 'twas past their power
    To work the others woe,
And loud the rescued passengers
    Taunted the vanquished foe.

All safely, in two minutes more,
    They reached their stopping place,
Then all stepped out with lightsome hearts,
    And went their several ways.
The Pirate Car was seen no more;
    The captured pirate team
The company kept (in harness) till
    The owner should redeem;
A thing the owner never did,
    Strange as the fact may seem.
The dauntless driver, who had proved
    So faithful in the strife,
They made, as I have since been told,
    An overseer for life
And now my tale has reached an end,
    To your regret, I wis;
May all the saints preserve us from
    A Pirate Car like this!

PANCAKES.

PANCAKES, flapjacks, slapjacks, griddle-cakes,
    no-matters, fritters,
All are names for the same delicious compound
    of buckwheat;
Though, as to that, the kind of the flour is not so
    essential,
Buckwheat being the best, but excellent cakes
    being made of
Oat, rye, Indian, wheat, the last either fine or
    unbolted.
Two points only are needful: the first that the
    cakes be served piping
Hot, and next that you eat them anointed with
    butter and syrup.
Try it once if you havn't, and sit in distended
    digestion,
After the gorgeous repast, as I am sitting this
    moment,
Sit and thank your stars that frying pans were
    invented,
Eke for the gift of the blooming buckwheat and
    sweet-blooded maples;
Last, but not least, for the golden butter,
    clovery-fragrant.
Thus, benighted beneath the beams of the
    scintillant North Star,
Caged by the Green Mountain walls and the walls
    of the far Adirondacks,
Under my feet Champlain, with its crooked level
    of whiteness,

Pine trees scenting the air, and the spunky
    thermometer's column
Tiptoeing up to freezing, in spite of the snow
    and the star-light,
Sitting thus, I say, emboldened by dinner
    and distance,
So have I ventured to sing to you, in
    hexameters daring,
Pancakes, flapjacks, slapjacks, griddle-cakes,
    no-matters, fritters.

THE CHESTNUT BELL.

HEAR the chuckle of the bells,
    Chestnut bells.
What a world of platitude their pertinence expels!
    How they twitter, twitter, twitter,
        In the office and the street,
    At the dull reiter-
        Ation of the bummer and the beat,
    Keeping time, time, time,
    In a sort of chronic rhyme,
To the antiquated pleasantries that pop into their shells,
    At the cogent cachinnation of the bells,
    At the jeering and the sneering of the bells.

THE TWELVE UNDERTAKERS OF BURLINGTON.

They were twelve undertakers,
  So round and red and jolly;
Each drove a brisk and healthy trade,
  And mocked at melancholy.

Said Mould to Spade one summer day,
  While merrily he laughed,
"Hast heard of this new medicine
  That's come to spoil our craft?

A cure-all has at last been found,
  A balm for every ill,
'T will heal the sick, and make the well
  Too tough for death to kill."

"And what might be the name," quoth Spade,
  " To such pretensions huge ? "
Said Mould, " They call it 'Potts's
  Protoplasmic Morbifuge.' "

Then loud they laughed, those reckless men,
  As 'twere a jest to live.
They went, and after them went Potts,
  The morbifugitive.

Next month the wretches met again,
  Quoth Spade to Mould, " How's trade ? "
" Alas ! " cried Mould, "some fearful blight
  Our fortunes doth invade.

This whole month long no funeral
  Has come to make me glad."
Quoth Spade, " My case exactly ;
  Affairs are getting bad.

The scoundrel Potts has done it all,
    Nobody now will die,
But all forget how thus they knock
    Our business into pie."

Said Mould, "We might as well give up,
    They have us on the hip.
How can we keep our hold on life,
    When men give death the slip?

But stop! our noble calling
    Must not so lightly cease.
There's yet a way the evil day
    To shove along a piece.

We two devoted craftsmen,
    With Clod, Nail, Dust, Worm, Crape,
Screw, Pickaxe, Headstone, Turf and Tears,
    May some of us escape.

The hour for lofty sacrifice
    Demands a patriot's will.
Let us draw lots to see who first
    Shall save our trade from ill.

The shortest lot betokens death,
    The longest will impart
The right to bury the deceased
    And give the trade a start."

The lots were laid, the lots were drawn;
    Headstone was first to fall,
And Mould must lay him in his grave,—
    Sad were the hearts of all.

But out spake dauntless Headstone,
  " Rejoice that I have died."
Then forth he drew a knife, and let
  Light into his inside.

Another month came round and saw
  Eleven despairing men.
There was no help, and so they drew
  The fatal lots again.

This time 'twas honest Worm that went.
  But little gain they found,
For, in a month from then, poor Clod
  Lay by him in the ground.

So, one by one, they passed away,
  And when a year had fled,
The wretched Spade was left alone,
  And, weeping, this he said:

" Alas! the noblest of all trades
  Now dies from off the earth.
In vain shall after ages mourn
  The loss of vanished worth;

And when men tire of toil, and throw
  Their worthless lives away,
No skillful hands shall lay their dust
  Beside its brother clay."

So saying, down into the grave
  He had already dug,
He stepped, and o'er him drew the earth
  To fill it tight and snug.

When all was neatly covered o'er
  He yielded up the ghost;
And then came Potts, and at his head
  Set up a wooden post;

Which he proceeded to bedeck
  With bills both great and small,
Telling how he had banished death
  From this terrestrial ball.

And now, if any one believes
  This tale I've tried to tell,
I shall be proud enough to wish
  It were not all a sell.

KING DEATH.

King Death was a grim old fellow,
  As he sat in his chair of state,
And emptied his goblet yellow,
  And spake in boastings great.

For he bragged that every acre
  On earth was his by right,
He had won them from their maker,
  In a fair and stand-up fight.

And King Death swigged and shouted,
  And cried as he drained his can,
"Ho, ho! it can't be doubted,
  I am monarch of earth and man."

And there he has sat and guzzled,
    Since ever the world was new,
Till men have been fooled and puzzled
    Into thinking his boasting true.

But Death, you're a fraud, and you know it,
    A coward, a craven, a cheat,
And full in your face I will throw it,
    Whenever we happen to meet.

THE DUDELING'S FATE.

It was a dainty dudeling,
    He dwelt in Avenue B.
By his big tall hat and his monstrous cane,
    You might be sure 'twas he.

He was his father's hope and pride,
    His mother's darling boy;
His name was Charles Augustus
    Fitz-William MacElroy.

No toil his hands e'er sullied;
    They were so white, I hope
To die if they weren't almost
    As white as Ivory Soap.

His eyes were large and lustrous
    And round as any O:
Like the two o's you've often
    Seen in Sapolio.

His nose was an example
  Of what a nose should be;
It took a sudden heavenward turn,
  Like early piety.

His chin (the mouth's front-door-step)
  Was a historic one,
Retreating swiftly, like our brave
  Defenders at Bull Run.

"How was he clad?" I'll tell you,
  As he would say, at *onth :*
His trousers were as tight as gold
  At ten per-cent a month.

His waistcoat was of creamy white,
  And snugger than the Scotch;
Across it hung a massive chain,
  On guard, if not on watch.

His coat,—I can't describe it;
  'Twas too divinely sweet;
Its fit was—epileptic;
  It came from Baxter street.

Last point of all, last two in fact,
  I mustn't fail to say,
Were those his toes, which matched his nose
  By being *retrousses.*

One morn this matchless masher,
  D. D., the Dude's Despair,
Set out between his hat and cane
  To pulverize the fair.

He saw not far before him
  A form of queenly grace;
He hurried by to turn around
  And look upon her face.

With eyeglass up he tried to turn.
  Woe worth the evil day!
His feet flew up as if they sought
  To tread the Milky Way.

They struck together with such force
  They never came apart;
Meanwhile his head below outspread
  Flat as a cranberry tart.

An ambulance was signalled for,
  Which took him to Bellevue.
He never looked, he never spoke,
  He doubtless never knew

The sad extent of all his woe;
  How his best hat was crushed,
His trowsers spoiled, his waistcoat soiled,
  His collar badly mushed.

He lay there in the hospital,
  And dried in every joint;
His head grew flat and flatter still,
  His feet came to a point.

And so he shriveled up and turned—
  Dear me! I really lack
Courage to tell you into what—
  Into a carpet tack.

I know it's so; because one night,
   As I was going to bed,
I stepped upon him,—or upon
   Some other tack instead.

I didn't swear (I never do),
   My joy was too sincere
To find the blamed tack had a head
   To stop its mad career.

But therewith against all mankind
   I vowed relentless hate;
With which in view I've penned for you
   This lay of the Dudeling's Fate.

WORK AND WAGES.

If there be any good
   In the Devil's reward,
We may wish it, of course,
   For the work of the Lord;

But the common demand
   Puts all on a level,—
Claims the pay of the Lord
   For the work of the Devil.

THE FISHERMAN.

A FISHERMAN sat on a wharf,
   And fished for tommy-cod,
His hook was baited with a clam,
   He fished without a rod.

Of flounders, rough-back, smooth-back too,
   And eels he caught full many,
But of the fish he strove to catch
   He could not capture any.

At last a mighty codfish came;
   He was not shy nor skittish,
He spied the clam, and said, "I am
   In luck now, like the British."

He made a grab and swallowed all,
   Bait, hook, snell and sinker,
Then struck out for the briny deep,
   As swift as thought from thinker.

The line was strong; its in-shore end
   By many a hitch was fastened
Unto the fisher's button-hole,—
   To hold it loose he durst n't.

A fishing pole would have allowed
   Time for deliberation,
But off went fish, and off went man,
   With like precipitation.

Down from the wharf the wretch was dragged,
   As 'twere by *habeas corpus*.
Men saw his coat-tails out at sea
   Bob like a breathing porpoise;

They heard a cry above the waves,
  "I've got him," faintly shouted,
But whether 'twas the man that spoke,
  Or else the fish, they doubted ;

And whether the fisherman swallowed the fish,
  Or the fish the fisherman,
I cannot tell, though there may be
  Somebody here that can ;

And now the doleful tale is told
  Of the fisherman and the cod ;
The moral is : Beware the fate
  Of those that spare the rod.

OUT WEST.

  Oh, the things that happen out west !
    It's frightful to think of the least ;
  But when you get out there, I'm blest
    If they all don't happen down east.

ANGELS' VISITS.

ANGELS' visits, though certainly few,
Have been more by hundreds than ever we knew,
And for every time that unaware
We have entertained such guest of air,
We have turned a hundred, unknown of course,
Bag and baggage from our doors.

RHYMES.

Sweet as honey from the skep,
Gentle Nanna, daughter of Nep,
Clad in robes of simple rep,
Forward came with modest step,
And bought a ticket for Dieppe.

SPRINGY.

There's an elasticity in the air
    That common folks call spring,
And big, fat robins everywhere
    Hop round and try to sing.

LOVE-PAINS.

If half the pains we take for love,
    Were spent in winning souls to Heaven,
There'd not be sinners left enough
    To give one minister a living.

THE LOVER'S OATH.

Ye stars that pepper-box the sky,
    Hearken unto me now;
Thou flitting, polyoptic fly,
    Bear witness to my vow.

THE POET.

The poet raves about the stars,
  And sings entranced of purling brooks;
But never gazes on the sky,
  And on the streamlet never looks.

THE THREE STAGES.

First I tried to live on faith,
  Which brought me small hilarity,
And then I tried to live on hope,
  And now I live on charity.

JONAH.

The whale had all he wanted of it,
When he had to swallow the prophet,
But we poor sinners catch it if we fail
To swallow Jonah *plus* the whale.

      .

AD SOCIUM.

Ecce! in media nocte,
Quo video te soci docte?
  Cum pulchra puella,
  Aliusque umbella,
Heu! video statu in hoc te.

HER MIND.

You had no mind, you said, and so,
   Since I have much, you had to flee me.
How flattering! but the truth I know
   Is that you had no mind to see me.

THE DEVIL.

"Love God and man, and thou shalt live."
   So comes the Savior's promise gracious.
But must we fear the devil too,
   To make that promise efficacious?

LIFE.

At morn, with stuffed and straining cars,
   The down-town train is crawling,
While, whizzing past, the up-train flies,
   With emptiness appalling.

At night the up-town train is crammed,
   No room by force or flattery,
While, empty as a beggar's hat,
   The down-train seeks the Battery.

www.ingramcontent.com/pod-product-compliance
Lightning Source LLC
Chambersburg PA
CBHW020842160426
43192CB00007B/747